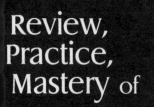

Review, Practice, Mastery of

COMMON CORE
ENGLISH LANGUAGE ARTS
STATE STANDARDS

Reviewers

Amy Barr • Park Hill School District • Park Hill, MO

Tracie Baumgartner • Valley View School District • Bolingbrook, IL

Barbara Burns • Lammersville Unified School District • Mountain House, CA

Karen Cooke • Cobb County School District • Marietta, GA

Amy Corr • Douglas County School District • Highlands Ranch, CO

Rachel Nichols • Lower Merion School District • Ardmore, PA

Arlene Peters • Orange County Public Schools • Orlando, FL

Brian Selling • Community Day Charter School • Lawrence, MA

Kim Sheehy • Sauquoit Valley Central Schools • Sauquoit, NY

Beverly Smith • Corona-Norco Unified School District • Ontario, CA

Colleen Thomas • Sandwich Public Schools • Sandwich, MA

Holly Walker • Whitman-Hanson Regional School District • Hanson, MA

© 2012 **Perfection Learning®**
www.perfectionlearning.com

11   12   13   14   15   PP   19   18   17   16

94524
ISBN-13: 978-0-7891-8298-2

Printed in the United States of America

To the Student

This book will help you review, practice, and master the English Language Arts Common Core Standards. Here are the steps to follow to use this book.

1. Take the Tryout Test over Reading Literature, Reading Informational Text, and Language and check your answers. Use the chart at the bottom of this page to find out your strengths and weaknesses in the areas covered. Remember the questions that are hard for you to answer. These will be the types of questions you need to work on the most.

2. Work through the units that follow the Tryout Test. The lessons in each unit review example items and provide a practice test based on the standards. Fill in the Keeping Score chart on page 130 as you complete each practice test.

3. After completing all the lessons, take the Mastery Test. Your score on this test will show your understanding of the Common Core Standards.

4. Work through the Writing Test Workhops section of the book. These lessons will help you learn how to read a writing prompt and how to get your ideas down on paper in a clear and organized manner.

Reading Literature	Tryout Test Items	Mastery Test Items
Unit One—Key Ideas and Details		
Lesson 1 Analysis and Inference	6, 7	12
Lesson 2 Theme and Summary	5, 13	4, 8
Lesson 3 Characters and Plot	1, 2	5, 6, 7
Unit Two—Craft and Structure		
Lesson 4 Word Choice	8, 9, 11, 12	9, 10, 11
Lesson 5 Structure and Point of View	3, 4, 10, 14	1, 3, 13
Unit Three—Integration of Knowledge and Ideas		
Lesson 6 Comparing and Contrasting Literature	15	14
Reading Informational Text	**Tryout Test Items**	**Mastery Test Items**
Unit Four—Key Ideas and Details		
Lesson 7 Analysis and Inference	25	19
Lesson 8 Main Ideas and Supporting Details	19, 26	21, 22, 23
Unit Five—Craft and Structure		
Lesson 9 Word Meanings	18	17, 29
Lesson 10 Text Structures and Purpose	17, 20, 21	18, 20, 28
Unit Six—Integration of Knowledge and Ideas		
Lesson 11 Integrating Information	27, 28, 29	24, 25
Lesson 12 Evaluating Arguments	30, 31, 32	30, 31, 32, 33
Language	**Tryout Test Items**	**Mastery Test Items**
Unit Seven—Pronoun Usage		
Lesson 13 Pronoun Case	33, 34	34
Lesson 14 Pronoun Shifts	35	34
Unit Eight—Conventions of Standard English		
Lesson 15 Capitalization, Punctuation, and Spelling	36, 37, 38, 39, 40, 41	35, 36, 37, 38, 39, 40
Lesson 16 Sentence Patterns	42	41
Unit Nine—Vocabulary		
Lesson 17 Word Analysis	16, 22	2, 15, 26
Lesson 18 Reference Materials and Multiple Meanings	23, 24	16, 27

Table of Contents

continued

Reading Informational Text

Language

Writing

Standards Key: RL = Reading Literature, RI = Reading Informational Text, L = Language, W = Writing, RH = Reading Standards for Literacy in History/Social Studies, RST = Reading Standards for Literacy in Science/Technical Studies

Note: A complete correlation of the Grade 6 Common Core Standards can be found in the Grade 6 Teacher Guide.

Tryout Test: Part 1

Directions: Read the passage and answer the questions that follow.

The Conversation Stealer

1 "He's such a little thief!" Liz said to her mother after school one day.

2 "Not another complaint about the new boy—what's his name, Manny?" Liz's mother asked. "Did he make off with your lunch or something?"

3 "Nope."

4 "Did he swipe your roller skates?"

5 "You mean *Rollerblades*. And no, he didn't."

6 "He must've nabbed your notebook and copied your homework."

7 "No, Mom. I didn't say he took a *thing*."

8 "Well, what did he steal?"

9 "He stole my *conversation*. Again. The fifth time this week!"

10 "What do you mean by saying he 'stole' your conversation? A conversation doesn't belong to anyone."

11 "A conversation can too belong to someone, and I'm sick and tired of Manny swiping mine. Why can't he find his own conversations, instead of making off with everyone else's?"

12 "I still don't get it."

13 "Well, today I was talking with Rachel about Rollerblading, when along comes Manny, who knows nothing about Rollerblading. He just stands there for a few minutes, not saying anything. Rachel and I are thinking, 'Did we ask you to join our conversation?' Finally, after he's eavesdropped long enough to catch on, he just barges in! Only, he's saying things that aren't quite right, so it kills the whole conversation, and Rachel walks off. Two minutes later, I hear Manny talking to Samir and Tasha about Rollerblading as if he's some kind of pro. I couldn't believe it!"

14 "Just a minute, Liz," her mother cautioned. "How do you know Manny isn't a Rollerblader too? Maybe he was interested in what you were talking about but was just too shy to say anything at first."

15 "I just know."

16 "It sounds like you're jumping to conclusions, Lizzy. Assuming things can get you into trouble. Besides, would it hurt to be nice? Why not include him in your conversation next time?"

17 "Oh, Mom, you just don't get it," Liz complained as she climbed the stairs to go to her room.

18 The next day at school, Liz saw Manny talking to Samir and Tasha again. "He's stealing another conversation, I'll bet," Liz thought. "I won't let him have the pleasure." She set out to crash the conversation and break it up, just to give Manny a taste of his own medicine.

19 However, as she got closer, she heard what Manny was saying, and it surprised her. He said that a Rollerblading competition was taking place after school that day at the park just down the street.

20 "How come no one told me about this?" she thought angrily. That was the last straw! Manny was going around stealing conversations and ruining them before the information could reach the people it was meant for in the first place! "Well, guess what?" Liz thought. "There is a new

conversation stealer in town." But if Manny stole conversations by infiltrating them, Liz's method would be more like wiretapping. After all, she had learned of the Rollerblading competition by eavesdropping. (They probably hadn't told her because they were afraid she'd win, she figured). By eavesdropping, she could out-steal Manny in a minute!

21 Liz began her mission at lunchtime. She went to a different lunch period than usual so her friends wouldn't interrupt her spy work. It was fun at first. She got some juicy gossip. Who knew, after all, that Crystal and Peter had played "mucho smooch-o" in the giant tires, or that Mrs. Schurr had given John Kopp detention for burping during the Pledge of Allegiance, or that Ms. Mench had actually cried when no one signed up for her bug-keeping club?

22 Eager for more, Liz changed tables but soon regretted it. The first thing she overheard was, "Have you ever noticed how that Liz Rios walks like a chicken? Come to think of it, she talks like a chicken too!" Everyone laughed.

23 Liz wanted to cry. "Walk like a chicken? Talk like a chicken!?" She couldn't believe anyone would be so cruel. That is, until she turned around quietly to see who was talking—it was the Cruel Crew. She half thought they'd seen her and were just trying to mess with her, but they were all facing the other way.

24 When they kept talking, Liz started to wish she'd never "gone undercover." The Cruel Crew decided to sabotage the Rollerblading competition at the park. They planned to boo the competitors, or make someone fall in the middle of a stunt. Liz did not want to know any of this! Now she had to sneak away or risk big trouble. Besides, how could she tell the others when she wasn't even supposed to know about the competition in the first place? And if the Cruel Crew found out she was the squealer, they'd make her life miserable.

25 Once she was out of the lunchroom, Liz spotted Ms. Mench. She had an idea. "Excuse me, Ms. Mench. It's about your activity club," she said. . . .

26 That afternoon, when the Cruel Crew showed up at the park, there were no Rollerbladers in sight. The Rollerblading competition had been moved to school grounds and was sponsored by Ms. Mench as part of her new activity club. Manny took first place. He was amazing, pulling off moves Liz had never even heard of. (So that's why some things he'd said during their first Rollerblading conversation hadn't made sense.) Manny was suddenly very popular. Everyone crowded around him. Liz didn't want to be the conversation stealer this time. She did want to be a participant, though. So, she walked right up to the group and chimed in, "Well, Ms. Mench, thanks again for sponsoring the competition. You've got twelve new members for your Rollerblading and bug-keeping club right here!"

27 Later that night Liz and her mom were talking. "Now do you see what I told you about jumping to conclusions?" her mom said.

28 "You were right," Liz conceded. "I had a lot of unraveling to do once I started assuming things. It would've been so much easier just to talk about these things directly, you know, in a good old-fashioned conversation."

1 This diagram shows the plot of the story.

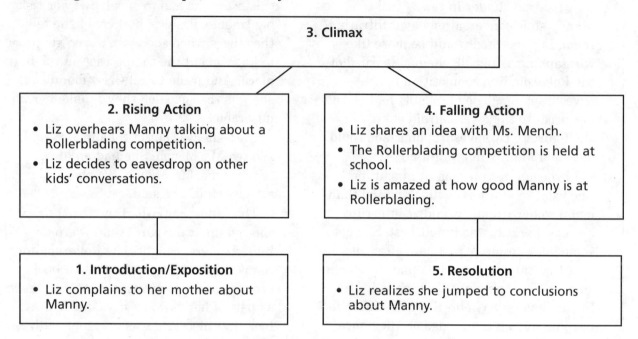

Which sentence belongs in the area marked "Climax"?

A Liz discovers that John Kopp has detention for burping.

B Manny barges in on Liz's conversations.

C Liz overhears a plot to sabotage the Rollerblading competition.

D Liz is angry that she didn't know about the Rollerblading competition.

2 How does Liz feel about her mother's advice at the beginning of the story?

A receptive

B resistant

C grateful

D enraged

3 You know this story is told in the third-person point of view because—

A it uses an outside narrator.

B Liz tells the story.

C Liz's mom tells the story.

D the narrator tells what happens to herself.

4 How does Liz's plan to eavesdrop on conversations contribute to the plot of the story?

A It results in her overhearing the Cruel Crew's plot to sabotage the Rollerblading competition.

B It causes her to hate Manny even more because he brags about his Rollerblading skills.

C It causes her to join the bug-keeping club.

D It results in her competing in and winning the Rollerblading competition.

5 A theme of this story is—

    A Don't judge others too quickly.

    B Those who steal should be punished.

    C Support your family members, even if they're wrong.

    D Become friends with your enemies.

6 How do Liz's actions in the story affect your opinion of her as a person? Use details from the story to explain your answer. (3 points)

_____

_____

_____

_____

_____

_____

_____

_____

7 How do you think Liz will treat Manny the next time he tries to join her conversation? Support your answer with details from the story. (3 points)

_____

_____

_____

_____

Directions: Read the poem. Then answer the questions that follow.

Summer Storm

Z-Z-Z-ZAP!
The sky cracks apart
Spilling shards of light
Over the landscape.

BOOM!
Clouds roil overhead—
Soon the sky is a sea
Filled with gray waves.

SPLAT!
Sudden rain soaks the soil
And washes summer's dust
From the parched earth.

www.photos.com

8   The word parched means—

   A sad.   **C** thick.

   B dry.   **D** muddy.

9   Reread these lines from the poem.

   Soon the sky is a sea

   Filled with gray waves.

   These lines are an example of—

   A a simile.   **C** an idiom.

   B a metaphor.   **D** personification.

10 Explain the importance of the first line of each stanza. How do these lines develop the main idea of the poem? (3 points)

_____

_____

_____

_____

_____

11 Which of the following words communicates a similar meaning and feeling as the word <u>cracks</u> in the first stanza?

   A opens

   B splits

   C pokes

   D explodes

12 The poet's use of the words <u>cracks</u>, <u>shards</u>, and <u>roil</u> communicate—

   A the gentle summer rain.

   B his anger at the weather.

   C the violence of the thunderstorm.

   D the sky on a sunny day.

Directions: Read this passage. Then answer the questions that follow.

Lost in the Storm

The thunder crashed, and lightning illuminated the sky. Torrents of rain poured down and flowed into Ella's eyes. With her heart pounding, she ran as fast as she could across the street and down an alley. Footsteps echoed behind her as she ran past a cardboard box and around a broken chair. She leapt over a pile of garbage without even noticing the meat scraps. Suddenly there was nowhere left to run. The alley was a dead end—Ella was trapped!

She cowered in the corner, with her ears flat against her head and her tail tucked between her legs. She turned as the dogcatcher approached slowly, speaking softly.

"It's okay, little pup. Just relax. I'm not going to hurt you."

The dogcatcher approached Ella slowly with his arms extended. He spoke in a gentle tone that made Ella feel a little less frightened. "Come here, pup," he said. Cautiously Ella crept toward him. He petted her on the head and then delicately slipped a collar around her neck. Ella tried to remain calm as the dogcatcher led her toward his truck.

Minutes later, Ella was sitting in a cage and riding along the dark, wet streets. The truck shook and shuddered on the potholed streets as lightning flashed overhead. Ella struggled to keep her balance. Soon the truck reached a large brick building with a sign that said "City Animal Shelter." After opening Ella's cage, the dogcatcher took her by the collar and led her through the back door, to yet another cage. Ella huddled against the wall and waited.

Ella was hungry and scared, but she tried to be brave. The night was long and lonely, and Ella missed the warm comfort of her home. She curled up in a tight ball and drifted off to sleep.

Ella was awakened when a woman walked into the room and flipped on the light. The rain had stopped, and the sun was gradually coming up. The woman spoke soothing words to all the animals as she filled their bowls with food and made sure that every animal had water. When the woman got to Ella's cage, Ella thumped her tail slowly. The woman smiled at Ella, scratched her behind the ears, filled her bowl with food, and then left the room.

Hours passed, and the sun sank below the horizon. Ella spent another long, lonely night at the animal shelter. The strangeness of her surroundings made her feel uneasy, and she slept very little.

The next morning, Ella awoke to the sound of familiar voices. She stood up and cocked her head, watching the doorway eagerly. Moments passed, and Ella began to wag her tail. Suddenly, Lisa and Fred ran into the room with their mother close behind them. Ella was rescued! The dogcatcher opened the cage door and she sprang out, wagging her tail. The children's mother explained to the

GO ON

dogcatcher, "When the storm started, Ella and I were on our way home. There was a big thunderclap, and she got spooked. She pulled out of her collar and disappeared. We looked everywhere. I'm so glad you found her!"

Ella barked excitedly as she bounded out to the family's car alongside Lisa and Fred.

13 Which paragraph best summarizes the passage?

A The dogcatcher approached Ella slowly and spoke in a gentle tone. When Ella came closer, he patted her on the head, then slipped a collar around her neck.

B Hours passed, and the sun sank below the horizon. Ella spent another long, lonely night at the animal shelter. She was uneasy and didn't sleep well.

C Ella ran off during a thunderstorm and got lost. The dogcatcher caught her and took her to the animal shelter. After two lonely nights in the shelter, Ella's family came to rescue her.

D Ella's heart pounded as she ran across the street and down an alley. She didn't stop until she realized she was trapped—there was nowhere to run!

14 All of the following details contribute to Ella's feeling of fear EXCEPT—

A the thunder and lightning during the rainstorm.

B the alley is a dead end.

C the footsteps approaching.

D the pile of meat scraps.

15 Compare and contrast the description of the weather in the poem "Summer Storm" on page 10 with the description of the storm in this passage. Support your answer with details from the story. (5 points)

_____

_____

_____

_____

_____

_____

_____

_____

_____

Take a break. Then go on to Part 2.

Directions: Read the passage and answer the questions that follow.

The Regions of South Africa

1   A lion lies on its back and basks in the warm desert sun. A baboon barks, and its cry echoes off the cliffs of a mountainside. A mongoose surveys the plains on the lookout for predators. These three animals all live in one of the world's most geographically diverse countries, South Africa. This country is home to an amazing variety of animals that live in three main <u>geographic</u> regions: the deserts, the mountain ranges, and the plateau.

Deserts

2   Deserts are an important part of South Africa's landscape. Large parts of two major deserts are within the country's borders. The Namib Desert lies along the Atlantic coast of South Africa and extends far into the country of Namibia. This desert is known for its towering sand dunes. It is an area that receives almost no rainfall. As a result, plant and animal life in the region has adapted to take water from coastal fog.

3   The Kalahari Desert lies in the northwest part of South Africa and extends into Namibia and Botswana. This region is covered with fine, red sand. The climate is hot and **arid** with very little rainfall. When rain does fall, grasses quickly sprout. Although the Kalahari is a harsh environment, many animals, including lions, hyenas, and antelope, thrive there. For example, the lions of the Kalahari can go for long periods without much water. These lions also have light-colored fur that helps them hide while stalking prey.

4   People live in the Kalahari too. The San people of South Africa are one of the oldest cultures in the world. They are a **nomadic** people who never settle in one area for very long. They travel throughout the desert, hunting, gathering food, and collecting water. They sleep in caves and rock shelters. They carry their belongings with them wherever they go.

Mountains

5   Long ago, the travels of the San brought them to another of South Africa's main geographic regions—the mountains. San rock paintings dating back more than 2 million years have been found in the Drakensberg Mountain Range. This ancient <u>range</u> runs along the southeastern part of South Africa. Some of its peaks rise more than 10,000 feet above sea level. Drakensberg means "dragon's mountain"

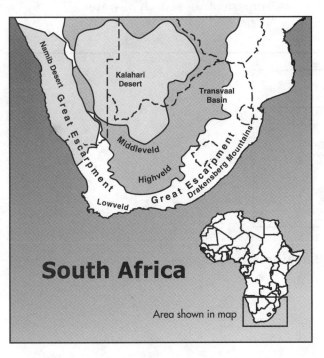

South Africa

Area shown in map

GO ON

in Afrikaans, one of South Africa's 11 national languages. The range is described in this way because the peaks resemble the points on a dragon's back. The Zulu people's name for this range means "the barrier of spears," also referring to the jagged mountaintops.

6   Baboons, sometimes called "dog-faced monkeys," live high in the cliffs of the mountains. Their barks can be heard over long distances. The baboons live in large troops of between 40 and 80 members. They **forage** for roots, seeds, and fruit. They also hunt insects and small animals.

Veld

7   The baboons' territory in part lies within a series of mountains and cliffs known as the Great Escarpment. The Great <u>Escarpment</u> serves as a natural boundary for South Africa's third distinct geographic region, the plateau. The **plateau** makes up roughly two-thirds of South Africa. There are three different zones within the plateau: the Highveld, the Middleveld, and the Transvaal Basin.

8   The Highveld is the largest of the three zones. It is located at a height between 4000 and 6000 feet above sea level. The area is characterized by flat-topped mountains and flat grasslands known as **velds**. The Middleveld is located in the northwestern part of the plateau, at altitudes of 2000 to 4000 feet. It has a desertlike climate. The rain that does fall is quickly absorbed by the area's sandy soil. All plants that grow there must be hardy enough to survive weeks or months with little water.

9   The Transvaal Basin is on the northeastern side of the plateau. The area is made up mostly of rolling hills and grasslands. It is home to Kruger National Park, a world-famous animal reserve.

10   One animal found in this dry, open region is the meerkat. Meerkats are a type of mongoose that lives in burrows and underground tunnels. They live throughout the grasslands in colonies of between 5 to 25 members. Members of the colony stand on their hind legs to watch for predatory birds.

11   South Africa consists of many varied lands, which contain many different climates, elevations, peoples, and animals. As the sun drops in the sky, the lion of the Kalahari rests, the baboon yawns and retires to its cliff-side cave, and the meerkat scampers off in search of water.

Glossary

arid	very dry
forage	search for food
nomadic	wandering
plateau	large, high, flat area of land
veld	open grassland

16 From the glossary definition, you can tell that **nomadic** people—

   A always live in deserts.

   B raise goats and sheep.

   C travel from place to place.

   D live in open grasslands.

17 Which organizational structure is used throughout most of this passage?

   A compare and contrast

   B chronological order

   C cause and effect

   D classification

18 Based on what you read, an <u>escarpment</u> is most likely—

   A a steep cliff.

   B a plateau.

   C below sea level.

   D a desert.

19 What is the main idea of this passage?

   A South Africa is diverse in terms of its geography, animals, and peoples.

   B South Africa is home to several large deserts.

   C Some parts of South Africa were inhabited more than 2 million years ago.

   D South Africa's climate is hot and arid with very little rain.

20 Paragraph 9 serves as a transition between the author's descriptions of—

   A the three zones of the Great Escarpment.

   B the animals of South Africa.

   C two geographic regions of South Africa.

   D Kruger National Park and the Kalahari Desert.

21 Which statement BEST describes the author's purpose for writing this passage?

   A to persuade readers to visit South Africa

   B to inform readers about South Africa's geography

   C to explain why desert people are often nomadic

   D to entertain readers with a story about South Africa

22 Which of the following BEST describes the origin of the word <u>geographic</u>?

   A The word comes from the Greek prefix *geo-*, meaning "earth," and the Greek root *graph*, meaning "write."

   B The word comes from the Greek prefix *geo-*, meaning "earth," and the Greek suffix *-ology*, meaning "science of."

   C The word comes from the Greek root *gram,* meaning "letter," and the Greek suffix *-ology*, meaning "science of."

   D The word comes from the Greek prefix *gen-*, meaning "race," and the Greek root *graph*, meaning "write."

23 As used in paragraph 5, the word <u>range</u> means—

    A a series of mountains

    B a place where shooting is practiced

    C a cooking stove

    D an open region over which livestock roam and feed

24 Finish the word association.

    BABOONS : CLIFFS :: meerkats :

    A tunnels

    B mongoose

    C fur

    D South Africa

25 In the first paragraph the author introduces the passage by—

    A telling stories about the people in South Africa.

    B describing animals that live in different regions of South Africa.

    C defining the geographical formations found in South Africa.

    D comparing the climate of South Africa to the rest of Africa.

26 Write a summary of the passage. Be sure to include the main idea and important supporting details from each section. (3 points)

_____

_____

_____

_____

_____

_____

_____

Directions: Study the Web site. Then answer the questions that follow.

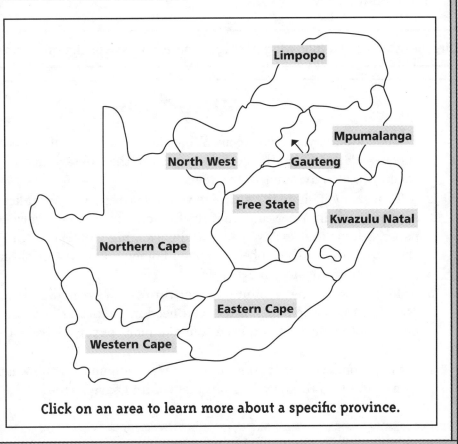

Visit South Africa

Welcome to the South Africa Tourism Web site. This is the best place to find information about visiting this magnificent country!

Featured Region *Western Cape* The Western Cape is an area no tourist should miss. Visitors will find gorgeous beaches, fine restaurants, ideal weather, many species of plants and animals, and an abundance of natural and human landmarks. No trip to South Africa would be complete without a stay in this special part of the country.

The region includes the southernmost point of South Africa, Cape Agulhus. Here you can experience spectacular ocean views. After all, this is where the Indian and Atlantic Oceans meet.

Click to go to...
Parks and Preserves
History and Culture
Geography
Plant and Animal Life
Climate and Weather
Getting to South Africa
Calendar of Events
Photo Gallery

While visiting the Western Cape, be sure to spend time at the area's major attractions.
* Table Mountain
* Cape Town
* Robben Island
* Cape Fortress
* Cape Agulhus

Address: http://www.visitsouthafricatoday.com

Back Forward Stop Refresh Home Mail Go

Limpopo

Mpumalanga

North West **Gauteng**

Free State

Kwazulu Natal

Northern Cape

Eastern Cape

Western Cape

Click on an area to learn more about a specific province.

GO ON

27 What is most likely the main purpose of the Web site?

   A to describe South Africa's geographic regions

   B to inform readers about the history of South Africa

   C to entertain readers with a story about South Africa's animals

   D to convince readers to visit South Africa

28 If you wanted to find out information about visiting Kruger National Park, you would most likely find this information—

   A in the section on velds from the article.

   B in the map of South Africa in the article.

   C by clicking the Web site link "Parks and Preserves."

   D by clicking the Web site link "Geography."

29 In which section of the Web site would you probably find similar information as you read in the article?

   A the link "History and Culture."

   B the link "Photo Gallery."

   C the map on the Web site.

   D the link "Geography."

Directions: Read the following passage, and then answer the questions that follow.

Why Recycle?

1   Look around your classroom. What do you see on bulletin boards, desktops, and shelves? Paper! From the books you read to the cafeteria menu you take home each week, you are surrounded by paper.

2   That's why it shouldn't surprise you to learn that paper takes up more room than anything else in American landfills. In fact, almost 40 of every 100 pounds of trash is paper. A lot of that is newspaper and packaging materials. But some of the paper that ends up in the trash can be completed homework, notes, or old magazines—the kinds of paper that *you* deal with every day.

3   Just knowing the amount of paper thrown away should convince you that it is essential to recycle paper. But if you need more facts, think about this: For every ton of paper that is recycled and used to make more paper, 17 trees DON'T need to be cut down!

4   So the next time you start to toss a piece of paper in the wastebasket, stop and think. Add it to the recycling bin instead and save a tree.

30 Which of the following reasons for recycling paper is explained in the first two paragraphs?

   A Recycling paper saves trees.

   B Much of the waste in landfills is paper.

   C Recycling saves the school money.

   D Recycling paper is easier than recycling other types of waste.

31 All of the following are facts from the passage except—

   A Almost 40 of every 100 pounds of trash is paper.

   B Paper takes up more room than anything else in American landfills.

   C You should recycle completed homework, notes, and old magazines.

   D For every ton of paper that is recycled and used to make paper, 17 trees don't need to be cut down.

32 What claim is made about recycling in paragraph 3? What evidence is given to support this claim? (5 points)

_____

_____

_____

_____

_____

_____

_____

_____

_____

Take a break. Then go on to Part 3.

Directions: Choose the correct pronoun for 33 through 35.

33 _____ went to the water park last summer.

  A Him and me

  B He and I

  C Him and I

  D He and me

34 I _____ am the person who called 911 when the fire started.

  A me

  B himself

  C mine

  D myself

35 Everyone brought _____ pets to walk in the parade.

  A his

  B her

  C their

  D his or her

Directions: Read each question and choose the best answer.

36 Complete the sentence below by choosing the word that is spelled correctly.

Measles used to be a common _____.

  A disease   **C** diseaze

  B diseeze   **D** dizease

37 Which title BEST completes the sentence below?

We will recite a poem called _____ for our parents.

  A "The Elephant And The Giraffe"

  B "the Elephant and the Giraffe"

  C "The Elephant and the Giraffe"

  D "The Elephant and the giraffe"

38 Which sentence is punctuated correctly?

  A Yesterday was our class picnic; and we went to the park.

  B The sun was shining, when we arrived.

  C Then the sky became overcast, and soon the rain began.

  D We grabbed our things. and we all ran for the bus.

39 Which sentence is punctuated correctly?

    A "Do you remember where the library is"? Darla asked.

    B "Do you remember where the library is? Darla asked."

    C Do you remember where the library is? Darla asked.

    D "Do you remember where the library is?" Darla asked.

40 Which sentence uses capitalization correctly?

    A My family is visiting New York city.

    B Dad said, "let's walk to Central park."

    C We started off by walking down Fifth Avenue.

    D I was tired by the time we got to the Park.

41 Which of the following sentences is punctuated correctly?

    A Maya's poem which was first published online won the poetry contest.

    B Maya's poem, which was first published online, won the poetry contest.

    C Maya's poem (which was first published online) won the poetry contest.

    D Maya's poem—which was first published online—won the poetry contest.

42 Edit the following passage by combining sentences. Vary sentence patterns to create an interesting paragraph. (3 points)

Last summer we went to the zoo. We saw lions. We saw hippos. We saw zebras. The lions live in the African grasslands area of the zoo. So do the zebras. The zoo re-created the animals' habitat. The African grasslands are filled with open grazing areas. There is a water hole in the center.

_____

_____

_____

_____

_____

_____

STOP

Points Earned/Total = _____ /60

Reading Literature Lesson 1

Analysis and Inference

Review the Standards (RL.6.1, W.6.9)

• **Analyze** a story
• Make an **inference** based on the text

Q: How do I **analyze** a story?

A: When you **analyze** a story, you break it down into its basic parts. You look at the plot, characters, and setting. Analysis of the story must be supported by evidence, or details, from the text.

Q: How do I make an **inference**?

A: An **inference** is a reasonable guess. If a question asks you to make an inference, you combine what the text says with what you already know.

 Try It

Directions: Read the passage. Then answer the questions that follow.

Rosie quickly changed after her morning swim practice. Glimpsing her reflection in the locker room mirror, she let out a groan. "Ugh!" Long strands of dark wavy hair hung limply around her face, making her look like a drowned rat. She considered drying her hair, but decided against it after looking at the clock.

As Rosie walked the four blocks from the pool to Roosevelt Middle School, her long, wet hair made her shiver. "At least it won't be that long tomorrow," she thought as she turned the red string around on her little finger. "I'm not going to forget my appointment at the hair stylist at 4 o'clock today!"

Rosie's last few yearbook pictures had been awful. One year the photographer had caught Rosie in mid-blink, making her look like she was half asleep. Another year Rosie asked her friend to braid her hair right before the picture. Little bunches of hair had stuck out everywhere, making her look like a strange space alien with dozens of short brown antennae.

Rosie was determined that tomorrow's picture would be better. Besides the red string, Rosie had a rubber band on her wrist so that she would remember to ask her sister if she could wear her blue cashmere sweater.

Rosie arrived at her classroom just as the final bell was ringing, but to her surprise, no one was there. She looked down the hall. Suddenly her first-period teacher rounded the corner and waved at her, "Hurry up, Rosie! We're in the cafeteria. Remember? It's picture day!"

---

1   Which of the following evidence from the text supports the conclusion that Rosie is forgetful?

   A Rosie's friends didn't remind her about school pictures.

   B She decides not to dry her hair before going to school.

   C She wears a rubber band to remind her to wear a blue sweater.

   D Rosie has not been happy with her school pictures in the past years.

2   What inference can you make about why Rosie doesn't dry her hair before school?

   A She doesn't have time before school.

   B She doesn't care how her hair looks.

   C She is going to dry her hair at school.

   D She wants her hair to be wet for school pictures.

   Example 1 asks you to think about which detail from the story supports the idea that Rosie is forgetful. Choice A can be eliminated because it is not found in the text. Choices B, C, and D are found in the text, but only choice C supports the idea that Rosie is forgetful. **Choice C** is correct.

   For **Example 2**, you must make an **inference** based upon the text. The story says that Rosie decides against drying her hair "after looking at the clock." We can infer that when she looks at the clock, Rosie decides she doesn't have time to dry her hair before school. **Choice A** is the correct answer.

◎ Try It On Your Own

3   All of the following details support the idea that Rosie is determined to take a good school picture EXCEPT—

   A she plans to get her hair cut before the picture.

   B she has picked out a blue cashmere sweater to wear.

   C she thinks this year's picture will be better.

   D she had the wrong day for school pictures.

4   At the end of the story, we can infer that Rosie feels—

   A relieved to have found out where her classmates are.

   B happy that she is getting her picture taken.

   C nervous about how her haircut will turn out.

   D unhappy to have her picture taken right then.

Theme and Summary

Review the Standard (RL.6.2)

- Determine a **theme**
- Provide a **summary**

Q: How do I find a **theme** of a story?

A: A **theme** of a story is a main idea. A good question to ask is, "What does the character learn from the conflict she is facing?"

Q: How do I **summarize** a story?

A: A **summary** of a story should include the setting, the main characters, and the major events explained in chronological order.

 Try It

Read the following selection. Then answer the questions that follow.

Two whole months, Emilio thought glumly, kicking a bottle cap all the way from his front stairs to the mini-mall. Emilio's family had just moved to Denver and Emilio had yet to meet any kids his own age. Now that his mother was occupied with his new baby sister, Emilio saw a long, tedious summer stretched ahead of him, relieved only by walks to the market to buy diapers.

Emilio was on his way out of the store when he noticed a brightly colored flyer lying near the cash register that read "Free Afternoon Summer Baseball Camp for Youths 12–14." Emilio took the flyer and showed it to his parents that evening.

"Sounds like fun and a good chance to meet friends," his father said.

"But Hector," said Emilio's mother, rocking Matilda, "the recreation center is all the way downtown. How will he get there?"

"I can take the bus, Mama," Emilio said quickly.

"You haven't taken the bus here before. What if you get lost? You don't know your way around yet." His mother's eyes were pools of worry.

"Now, Rosa. He's not a little baby anymore. When I was his age, I rode buses all over. Besides, if he's going to get around in this city, he has to learn to take buses, doesn't he?" Emilio's mother frowned, but she knew that her husband was right.

The next time Emilio went to the market, he asked the store owner how to get to the recreation center by bus. The store owner pointed out the stop where Emilio would catch his first bus and explained that he would have to get off at Park Avenue and transfer to the 25 bus, which would take him to the rec center.

On Monday, equipped with his fielder's glove and cap, Emilio left early so that he wouldn't be late. His mother and baby sister walked him to the bus stop.

"Now, you're sure you have enough money?" his mother asked. "You'll need $2.25 to get there and $2.25 to get back, and be sure to ask for a transfer. Call me if you get lost. I'll find a way to come get you." She looked at Emilio sternly for a moment, but Emilio understood that it was just how she expressed her concern for him.

"I'll be fine, Mama. Don't worry. I'll be back by six o'clock, okay?" Although Emilio felt a little nervous himself, he didn't want his mother to see it.

As the bus approached, Emilio hugged his mother. As he boarded the full bus, Emilio felt shy looking into the sea of strange faces, so he took the one empty seat near the driver. At the next stop, however, a snowy-haired woman got on the bus, and the driver turned around and pointed to a blue sign over Emilio's head: "Front seats must be vacated for seniors and persons with disabilities."

www.photos.com

Emilio stood up quickly. "Sorry," he said, blushing. The old woman just smiled at Emilio and said, "Why, that's very kind of you, young man."

Since there were no other seats available, Emilio stood in the aisle, clutching a metal pole to steady himself. At one moment, the bus rounded a corner, and he nearly fell into a woman holding a baby. Gradually, he got used to the movement of the bus.

After about 20 minutes, Emilio saw the Park Avenue street sign. He wasn't sure how to ring the bell to get the bus to stop, but thankfully another passenger had to get off too, and Emilio saw her pull a cord hanging along the upper part of the windows. As Emilio stepped off the bus, he saw that his timing was perfect. The 25 bus was pulling up on the opposite corner. This time Emilio was able to find a seat toward the front of the bus. Almost there, he thought, staring out the window at the machine shops and fences. This wasn't so hard after all.

Then Emilio noticed something was wrong. Instead of getting smaller, the street addresses were getting bigger. How was that possible? Suddenly it dawned on him: he'd caught the bus on the wrong side of the street! He could get off, but now that he'd used his transfer, he would have to buy another ticket to go back in the other direction. Realizing that his only chance was to try to explain his situation to the driver, he slowly made his way to the front of the bus.

GO ON

"Excuse me," Emilio said tentatively, as the driver maneuvered between a moving van and a mail truck.

"Yeah?" said the driver, keeping his eyes focused on the traffic ahead.

"Uhhh . . . I'm going the wrong direction and I gave you my transfer and . . ."

"Where are you going?" the bus driver interrupted.

"To the Denver Municipal Recreation Center."

"Well, you're in luck," the driver said. "This is the 25 Downtown Loop. You can just stay onboard until we circle back around town. It will take about 45 minutes. Or, if you're in a hurry, I"ll give you another transfer to catch a bus back."

Emilio checked his watch. He had an hour until camp started. "Thanks, I guess I'll stay on." He settled back down into his seat and watched the city scenes appear and disappear as if he were watching a movie. If baseball camp turns out okay, he thought, it won't be such a boring summer after all.

---

1 Which of the following is important and should be included in a summary of the story?

  A Emilio and his family have moved to Denver.

  B Emilio asks the manager at the grocery store which bus he needs to take to get to the rec center.

  C Emilio's dad says that he used to ride the bus when he was Emilio's age.

  D In order to attend a baseball camp downtown, Emilio rides the bus by himself for the first time.

2 Which sentence below best communicates the theme of the story?

  A Practice what you preach.

  B Trust your parents to know best.

  C Moving to a new city is hard.

  D It is good to try new things.

Example 1 asks you to think about which choice is an important detail of the story. Choice A leaves out the main idea of Emilio riding the bus. Choices B and C include minor details that should not be included in a **summary**. **Choice D** includes an important detail about the story.

For **Example 2** you need to understand a **theme**, or a central idea of the story. To identify a theme, you need to think about the conflict, characters, and plot of the story.

Conflict: *Emilio is riding the bus for the first time.*

Character: *Emilio is nervous, but determined to get to camp.*

Plot: *Emilio wants to go to baseball camp, so he takes the bus downtown. Although he transfers to the wrong bus, he finds that he can still make it to the camp on time.*

We can determine that the best answer is **choice D**.

◎ Try It On Your Own

3 Write a summary of the story on the lines below. Include the main idea and any important supporting details. (3 points)

_____

_____

_____

_____

_____

4 Based upon Emilio's actions and the outcome of the story, another theme of the story might be—

A the importance of being honest.

B learning to be independent.

C the positive benefits of sports.

D the benefits of riding the bus.

Reading Literature Lesson 3

Characters and Plot

Review the Standard (RL.6.3)

- Describe how the **characters** respond and change
- Describe the **plot**

Q: How can I figure out how **characters** respond and change?

A: Think about how you would describe the **characters** based upon what they say and do. Describe the characters based upon how they respond to problems or conflicts in the story. Then consider what the character is like at the end of the story. How has the character changed during the story?

Q: How do I describe the **plot**?

A: Plot is the series of events or episodes that make up a story. Often plot is described using the following diagram.

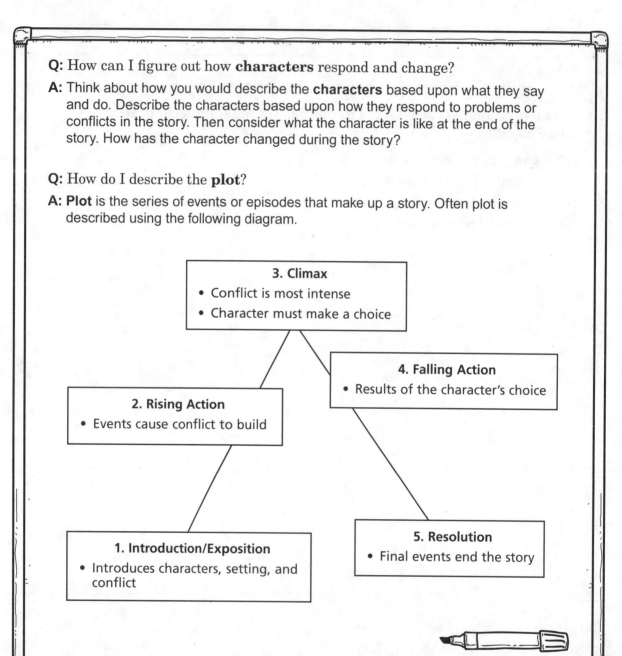

3. Climax
- Conflict is most intense
- Character must make a choice

4. Falling Action
- Results of the character's choice

2. Rising Action
- Events cause conflict to build

1. Introduction/Exposition
- Introduces characters, setting, and conflict

5. Resolution
- Final events end the story

Read the following story and answer the questions that follow.

"This looks like a good spot for our camp." Kyle's dad turned off the dirt road and parked the car next to a small juniper tree. Kyle, a lanky twelve-year-old with wild brown hair, jumped out of the car and scrambled up a nearby boulder to get a better view. Fists on his hips, he surveyed the landscape with intense concentration. The sun setting over the Chuska Mountains cast a golden-red glow over the valley. Off to the east, red-brown sandstone cliffs rose up from the valley floor like an ancient fortress.

"I've got to remember this," Kyle thought. Tomorrow they would be heading home to Chicago. Even after ten days of camping in the Southwest, he was eager to see more. Kyle loved everything about New Mexico. He was amazed by the rock formations, and he loved the Native American communities he and his dad had visited.

Kyle had a fascination with Native Americans of the Southwest. He and his grandfather loved to go to the library on Saturday mornings and find books about the Southwestern cultures. When Kyle turned ten, Grandpa gave him a replica of a Navajo arrowhead. Since then Kyle had dreamed of someday finding a real one.

The next morning, Kyle woke up early. He quickly got dressed and rolled up his sleeping bag. He wanted to enjoy every minute of his last day in New Mexico. Kyle took milk and cereal out of the cooler, and the clanking of spoons soon woke his dad.

After they had eaten breakfast and packed everything up, Kyle's dad pulled out a map to figure out their route back home. Kyle stood and looked around. To either side of him sharp peaks jutted up from the valley, forming jagged silhouettes against the clear blue sky. To the south lay red, flat-topped mesas.

"Grandpa would love this," he thought. Grandpa had lived in Chicago all his life, but as a young man, he had traveled through the Southwest on a road trip. Of all the places he visited, he liked New Mexico best. "The Land of Enchantment," he called it.

www.photos.com

Kyle and his grandfather had planned this trip out West together, but a few weeks before they were set to go, Grandpa fell. He was steadily improving, but the doctor said that he wasn't strong enough to go camping. Kyle had wanted to cancel the trip, but his grandpa had insisted that Kyle and his dad go without him.

"What are you thinking about?" asked his dad, folding up the map.

"Grandpa," Kyle said. "I wish he could see this again." Kyle had taken plenty of photographs, but he doubted that they could capture the beauty of this land. And they would not make up for Grandpa's disappointment about missing the trip.

"You'll have lots of stories to take back to Grandpa," his dad said. "Let's take a quick look around before we head out." The two set off in the direction of a dry creek bed. The cracked brown earth where the water had once flowed looked like pieces of broken pottery.

Near the edge of the creek bed a lizard suddenly darted out from behind a rock. Kyle knelt down to take a closer look, but the startled lizard scurried away.

Then something else caught Kyle's eye. A small tip of white rock jutted up where the lizard had been just seconds before. Kyle carefully dug it up and brushed it off. It was a piece of flint in the shape of an arrow, with two points at the bottom.

"Hey, Dad!" he called out. "Look what I found."

"Well, I'll be . . . ," said his dad as he walked up. "Looks like you've found an arrowhead."

"How old do you think it is, Dad?" Kyle asked, turning it over in his hand.

"Well, if it's real—and it probably is out here—it could be 150 years old or more."

"Wow. I can't wait to show Grandpa."

"I hate to break the news to you, Kyle, but we're on state land. That means that we're not supposed to take away anything that we find here."

Kyle's heart dropped. "But it was just lying here. Would anybody miss it?"

"I'm just telling you the law," his dad said, shrugging. "Besides, if everybody took what they found here, soon there would be nothing left for anyone else to discover. You know," he added, patting Kyle on the back, "we should probably get going." He turned and headed back in the direction they had come.

Kyle stood with the arrowhead in his hand, feeling the smooth, flat surface and the sharp edges. He wanted so badly to slip the arrowhead into his pocket, to take back a real piece of New Mexico to share with his grandfather. He wondered what his grandfather would do if he were here. "Grandpa would leave it for someone else to discover," he thought. In that moment, Kyle realized that what he shared with his grandfather was bigger than anything he could take home in his pocket.

Kyle knelt down to place the arrowhead in the dirt where he found it. Then he slowly walked back to the car.

---

1   Which word BEST describes Kyle?

   A angry

   B thoughtful

   C bored

   D scared

2 What conflict does Kyle face in this story?

  A He wants to take the arrowhead but knows he shouldn't.

  B He and his father are fighting all the time on their trip.

  C He doesn't want to leave New Mexico to go home.

  D His grandfather refuses to come to New Mexico with Kyle and his father.

Example 1 asks you to think about Kyle's **character**. Consider what Kyle does and says during the story, and then read the answer choices. There is no support in the story to suggest that Kyle is angry, bored, or scared. We do know that Kyle thinks about his grandfather and considers what his grandfather would do several times during the story. The correct choice is **B**.

For **Example 2**, you must think about the central conflict of the story. The events of the story lead to the climax of the story in which Kyle must decide whether to keep the arrowhead. The best choice is **A**.

◎ Try It On Your Own

3 What lesson does Kyle learn from his conflict about whether to keep the arrowhead? How would you describe Kyle at the end of the story? Support your answer with evidence from the text. (3 points)

_____

_____

_____

_____

_____

4 What event causes Kyle to want to keep the arrowhead he finds at the state park?

  A Kyle and his dad are camping in the Southwest.

  B Kyle and his grandfather went to the library and found books on the Southwestern cultures.

  C Kyle's grandfather had given him a replica of a Navajo arrowhead.

  D Kyle's grandfather fell and hurt himself.

5 Which of the following sentences belongs in the area marked "Resolution"?

3. Climax
- Kyle's father tells him he can't keep the arrowhead.

2. Rising Action
- Kyle wishes his grandfather was well enough to go camping.
- Kyle and his father take a walk.
- Kyle finds an arrowhead.

4. Falling Action
- Kyle thinks about what his grandfather would do.

1. Introduction/Exposition
- Kyle and his father are camping in New Mexico.

5. Resolution

A Kyle puts the arrowhead back on the ground.

B Kyle sees a lizard.

C Kyle dreams of finding an arrowhead.

D Kyle and his father arrive home in Chicago.

Test-Taking Tips

1 Go back to the story to find evidence to support analysis about the text.

2 To make an inference, think about what the text says and what you already know from your own experiences.

3 Questions about theme are asking you to explain the main idea, or the message, of the story. Consider the central conflict of the story, how the main character responds to the conflict, and how the conflict resolves.

4 To answer questions about summarizing a text, think about the main idea and the important details. Do not include minor details.

5 To answer questions about how a character changes in the story, compare what the character says and does at the beginning and at the end of the story.

6 To answer questions about plot, ask yourself, "What happens at the beginning of the story? In the middle? At the end? What conflict is the character facing?" Consider how events in the story cause other events to happen.

Go for it!

Unit One Practice Test

Estimated time: 18 minutes

Directions: Read the following passage, and then answer the questions that follow.

1 "Why did I get myself into this mess?" Rani thought, as she tried to steady herself after her third awkward fall on the ice. Her tired ankles wobbled, and her legs slid forward one moment, backward the next, and sometimes in both directions at once.

2 A pair of skaters swooshed gracefully by her, their skates cutting neatly into the ice. Rani watched them enviously, wishing she could skate like that. They made it look so simple!

3 Earlier that day, Rebecca had approached her in the hallway. "Hey, Rani," Rebecca called. "A group of us are going skating tonight. Want to come?"

4 "Sure. Sounds fun," said Rani casually. She tried to act cool, but she couldn't stop a warm blush from creeping onto her cheeks. She turned to shove some books in her locker in order to mask her embarrassment. Rani's family had just moved to town three weeks ago, and she was having trouble making friends at her new middle school. Rebecca and her friends were the most popular kids in the sixth grade.

5 "You don't need lessons, do you? We would have to go early for those," Rebecca explained.

6 "No, I'll be fine. I used to skate a lot when I was younger," answered Rani.

7 "Great. My mom and I will pick you up around 7:30."

8 It wasn't until they pulled up to the rink and Rani saw the words "Fun on Ice" that she realized she had gotten herself into trouble.

9 "Why didn't I ask Rebecca what kind of skating?" Rani groaned, as she brushed the powdery ice off her pants after yet another clumsy wipeout. She had been roller-skating plenty of times, but she quickly learned that ice-skating was entirely different.

www.photos.com

10   Frustrated, she moved to the railing and clutched it with relief. It wasn't so much that she was afraid of falling, but she had so hoped to impress the other kids and make new friends. Instead she was making a fool of herself with all her slipping and sliding, while they were zipping around the rink as if they had been born on ice.

11   Just then she heard laughing and looked up to see Rebecca weaving a figure eight around her friends, Kevin and Jennifer. "Every other person here skates better than I do," thought Rani gloomily. "These kids will think I'm a freak." The other day when she'd scored a point in "Math Olympics," Kevin and Jennifer had given her high fives. But tonight she was earning only low zeros.

12   "I may as well turn in my skates. I've had it," she sighed. Suddenly she felt a firm grip around each of her arms. Before she realized what was happening, Rani found herself whooshed out to the center of the rink. Kevin and Rebecca held her safely upright. She was skating—fast! Her legs didn't feel like her own. In disbelief she cried, "Guys, take me back to the rail! I can't ice-skate."

13   "Sure you can," Kevin said, grinning at her. "All you need are a few lessons from friends."

1   Based on paragraphs 9 and 10, we can infer that Rani—

   A has never ice-skated before.

   B is not good at sports.

   C lives in a warm climate.

   D has taken roller-skating lessons.

2   Which of the following BEST summarizes the story?

   A Rani is new at school. Rebecca asks her to go skating. Rani agrees to go, and she learns that ice-skating is much more difficult than roller-skating. She decides to turn in her skates.

   B Rani agrees to go skating with some new friends from school. When they pull up to the ice rink, Rani knows she is in trouble. She watches her friends zip around the ice as if they were born on ice.

   C Rani is new at school. Rani goes ice-skating and falls down a lot. She remembers how her friends reacted when she scored a point in the "Math Olympics." Rani's friends take her out to the center of the rink.

   D Rani agrees to go skating with some new friends from school. She finds out they are going ice-skating, not roller-skating. Rani is embarrassed because she can't ice-skate. Her new friends offer to help her learn.

3 This diagram shows the plot of the story.

```
                    ┌─────────────────────────────────┐
                    │          3. Climax              │
                    │ • Rani decides to turn in her   │
                    │   skates.                       │
                    └─────────────────────────────────┘
```

2. Rising Action
- Rani realizes it's an ice-skating rink.
- Rani keeps falling down.

4. Falling Action
- Kevin, Rebecca, and Rani skate together.

1. Introduction/Exposition
- Rani is a new girl at school.
- Rebecca invites Rani skating.

5. Resolution

Which sentence belongs in the box marked "Resolution"?

A Rani learns she will be ice-skating, not roller-skating.

B Rani scores a point in the "Math Olympics."

C Rani falls down for the last time.

D Rani realizes that she has made new friends.

4 At the rink, Rani can BEST be described as—

A fearless.   **C** discouraged.

B bored.   **D** cheerful.

5 Describe how Rani changes throughout the story. Be sure to give evidence from the story to support your conclusions. (3 points)

_____

_____

_____

_____

_____

6 Which sentence BEST expresses the story's theme?

A Sometimes all you need is a little help from friends.

B Ice-skating can be dangerous.

C Teaching someone to skate is hard work.

D Pretending to be clumsy can help you make friends.

STOP

Points Earned/Total = _____/8

Reading Literature Lesson 4

Word Choice

Review the Standards (RL.6.4, L.6.5.a)

- Determine the meaning of **figurative language**
- Understand **connotation** and **denotation**
- Analyze word choice and **tone**

Q: What is **figurative language**?

A: Figurative language suggests something other than the literal meaning of the words. This chart explains a few types of figurative language.

Figurative Language	Definition	Example
Simile	comparison using *like* or *as*	He ate like a wild beast.
Metaphor	comparison that says something *is* something else	The howling wind is a roaring lion.
Personification	giving human qualities to something that is not human	Flowers danced in the wind.
Idiom	group of words with a meaning that is different from the literal meaning of the individual words	It was raining cats and dogs.
Hyperbole	exaggeration used for effect	I could eat a horse!

Q: What is the difference between the **denotation** and **connotation** of a word?

A: A word's **denotation** is its dictionary definition; its **connotation** is suggested meaning which has a positive or negative emotion associated with it.

Q: What is the difference between **tone** and **mood**?

A: Tone has to do with the writer's attitude toward what he is writing. Some examples of tone are serious, humorous, sarcastic, informal, or formal. **Mood** is how the piece makes the reader feel. The writer's choice of words communicates both the tone and the mood of the story.

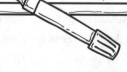

Directions: Read the following poem and answer the questions that follow.

The Highwayman

The wind was a torrent of darkness among the gusty trees,
The moon was a ghostly galleon tossed upon cloudy seas,
The road was a ribbon of moonlight over the purple moor,
And the highwayman came riding—
Riding—riding—
The highwayman came riding, up to the old inn-door.

www.photos.com

1 Identify the figurative language used in the phrase "The road was a ribbon of moonlight over the purple moor." Then explain its meaning. (3 points)

_____

_____

_____

2 Which of the following has the same connotation as the words *torrent* and *gusty*?

   A a summer breeze

   B a tornado

   C a puff of wind

   D a rush of wind

3 Describe the mood of the poem. Give two examples of words or phrases from the text that create this mood. (3 points)

_____

_____

_____

4 The words used in the passage create what kind of tone?

   A serious

   B humorous

   C sarcastic

   D informal

There are two parts to answering **Example 1**, so be sure to complete both parts. First, you should identify the **figure of speech** used. The figure of speech is a metaphor because the author is saying the road _was_ a ribbon of moonlight. From the words used, we can conclude that the road twists over the moor and shines in the moonlight and looks like the silky fabric of a ribbon.

Good: _This phrase is a metaphor that compares a road to a ribbon of moonlight. The phrase means the road was reflected in the moonlight as it wove through the countryside._

A poor answer will incorrectly identify the figure of speech and will not explain what the phrase means.

Poor: _This phrase is hyberbole. It exaggerates how the road looks in the moonlight._

For **Example 2**, you must consider the **connotation** of the words _torrent_ and _gusty_. You may not be as familiar with the word _torrent_, but you probably know that a gusty wind blows very hard and then slows down before blowing hard again. The answer is **choice D**.

Example 3 asks you to describe the **mood** of the piece. The words used to describe the ghostly moon and the wind in the trees create a mood of mystery and suspense.

Good: _The mood of the poem is mysterious and suspenseful. One detail that creates this suspenseful mood is the wind rushing through the "gusty trees." Another detail is the description of the moon that looks like a "ghostly galleon."_

Poor: _The mood of the poem is happy. A man is going for a ride on his horse._

To answer **Example 4**, you should think about the **tone**, or the author's attitude toward the writing. The descriptive words used are carefully chosen to create a serious tone, or **choice A**.

Read the following poem. Then answer the questions that follow.

My little brother BAWLS,
The dog HOWLS at neighborhood cats,
The TV BLARES loudly from the den.
I grab my coat and a scarf and rush
Outside, to the winter night.
The street is empty, quiet,
Except for the sound of snow
Crunching beneath my feet
And the wind whispering in my ear.
I hear nothing but the night's mysterious music.
Around me bare branches hunch over like old men.
Cozy fires glow inside tiny houses.
As snow falls, everything becomes quiet and still, like a prayer.
Little snowflakes dance around the streetlights,
Twisting and pirouetting slowly to the ground.
I circle back to my front door,
Determined to take the quiet of the night inside with me.

5 The line "And the wind whispering in my ear" is an example of a(n)—

  A simile.

  B metaphor.

  C personification.

  D idiom.

6 Which of the following gives the BEST explanation of the meaning of the line "Around me bare branches hunch over like old men"?

  A The tree branches were very old.

  B The curved tree branches remind the author of old men who are bent over.

  C There were old men walking in the snow.

  D The tree branches would make good canes for old men who walk bent over.

7 Do the words BAWLS, HOWLS, and BLARES have positive or negative connotations? How do these words communicate the meaning of the poem? (3 points)

_____

_____

_____

_____

_____

_____

_____

_____

_____

_____

_____

_____

8 The overall mood of the poem is BEST described as—

A suspenseful.

B peaceful.

C sad.

D angry.

9 Which word BEST describes the tone of the poem?

A formal

B informal

C humorous

D sarcastic

Reading Literature
Lesson 5

Structure and Point of View

Review the Standards (RL.6.5, RL.6.6)

- Analyze how a sentence or stanza fits into the overall structure of a text
- Analyze how a sentence or stanza develops the **theme**, **setting**, or **plot**
- Explain how an author uses **point of view**

Q: How do I determine how a part of a story or poem contributes to the whole text?

A: Some questions will ask you to think about how a certain sentence, paragraph, or line contributes to the whole text. Think about what the theme of the story is, then ask yourself: *How does this detail contribute to the theme of the story?*

Q: How do writers use **point of view**?

A: Point of view is related to the person who is telling the story. Study the following chart.

Point of View	Description
First person	narrator is a character in the story; uses words like *I*, *my*, and *me*
Third-person limited	narrator is someone outside the story who tells the thoughts of only one character; uses *he*, *she*, and *they*
Third-person omniscient	narrator is someone outside the story who tells the thoughts and feelings of all characters; uses *he*, *she*, and *they*

First-person point of view allows the writer to help the reader get inside the head of one character. Writers use third-person point of view when they want to give a broader perspective of how several characters view the events of the story.

GO ON

Read the following poem. Then answer the questions that follow.

The following poem is about a girl who gains strength from memories of her grandmother.

Plowing the Past

1 Lila trudged behind the mare,
Woolen dress hem bare, stained brown.
She is bound by leather to mare and plow.

Her hand gripped reins and pulled right.
5 Horse turned, leather groaned,
Plow sowed yet another vein.

"Two more rows now," Lila sighed.
Wiping sweaty brow, she stumbled.
"Best get on with it, Lila Mae," her mother called.

10 Across the field, Lila saw her mother's hands,
Red-streaked from cotton bolls that <u>nicked</u> and <u>nibbled</u>.

"Why tread the field in <u>endless</u> rows," Lila wondered,
"While meadows sway over yonder,
Calling me to play?"

15 But her hand gripped reins and pulled left.
Horse turned, leather groaned.
Plow sowed yet another vein.

Her grandmother had told her not to cry.
"No need for nonsense out here," she'd said.
20 "Now <u>gather your grit</u> and do your chore."
With <u>hands like un-ironed linen</u> she waved toward the field.

Lila did as she remembered.
Hand gripped reins and pulled right.
Horse turned, leather groaned.
25 Plow sowed yet another vein.

1 The poem is written in—

   A first-person point of view.

   B third-person point of view.

   C both first- and third-person point of view.

   D neither first- nor third-person point of view.

2 Which stanza BEST describes the conflict Lila faces?

   A stanza 1 (lines 1–3)

   B stanza 3 (lines 7–9)

   C stanza 5 (lines 12–14)

   D stanza 8 (lines 22–25)

3 Explain how stanza 7 (lines 18–21) is important to the resolution of the conflict Lila is facing. (3 points)

_____

_____

_____

_____

_____

_____

Example 1 asks you to identify the **point of view** of the story. The speaker is not a character in the story. The narrator uses the pronouns *she* and *her*. The correct answer is **choice B**.

To answer **Example 2**, you must think about how each **stanza** develops the **conflict**. Reread each stanza and think about which one explains the conflict, or problem, Lila is facing. Stanza 5 describes Lila's struggle with having to work hard when she wants to play. **Choice C** is the correct answer.

Before answering **Example 3**, reread stanza 7. In this stanza, Lila remembers her grandmother's encouragement to be strong even when things are tough. Her grandmother's words motivate her to not give up. This stanza results in the resolution of the conflict so that in stanza 8 Lila keeps plowing the field. A good response might look something like this:

Good: *In stanza 7, Lila remembers how her grandmother encouraged her to be strong and work hard. This motivates Lila to keep on plowing the field instead of going out to play. Stanza 7 explains the reason Lila keeps working and doesn't give up and leads to the resolution of the conflict in stanza 8.*

A poor answer would give incorrect information, not focus on the point of the question, or would not refer to specific details from the text.

Poor: *Lila is a girl from the past who must work in the field. Working in the field is difficult. Lila's grandmother makes her work in the field and won't let her play. I wouldn't like to live in the past and have to work all day.*

This passage is an excerpt from a novel that is set in France during World War II. Nazi soldiers have just shot down a British plane, but the narrator has seen a parachute. She has gone to find the pilot before the Nazis do.

from *A Light in the Sky*
by Cynthia Mercati

1   A sharp, bright moon had come out from behind the clouds. I used that to guide my steps, but I had to make sure I wasn't seen. I crouched low and kept in the shadows, looking around me all the time.

2   I branched off the road to cut across a meadow. Then I followed the footpath that led me into the Normandy woods. Maybe the Nazis didn't know the downed pilot had bailed out, but it was more likely that they did. At any time, from anywhere, they might appear.

3   I strained my ears for the sound of their cars or dogs. But now, after the noise of the battle, the silence was so deep it seemed to swallow me up.

4   Soon there was an ache in my side, and my heart was thudding. But I didn't slow my pace.

5   If the Nazis were on the lookout for the pilot, I had one advantage. I had played in these woods for years. I knew every inch of the ground by heart.

6   I knew exactly where the path dipped down and where it rose again. I knew where the strangely shaped dead tree stood. The ghost tree, we called it. I knew where the pine trees got so thick you couldn't walk through them and where they thinned out again. This was my home, and I knew it as well by night as I did by day. But to the Germans, these dark woods would be a forbidding place.

7   I was coming closer and closer to the location where I thought the parachute had come down. It was a small clearing where my friends and I often lit a bonfire on summer nights.

8   "Please," I whispered as I ran, "please don't let the Nazis get there first!"

9   Then just a few feet away, I saw the clearing. I was right! This was exactly where the pilot had bailed out! His parachute was caught on the branches of a tree.

10   I have to get that down, I thought. The whiteness of it is like a light, leading the Nazis right to this spot.

11   Suddenly I froze in my tracks. I covered my eyes with both hands. A pencil-thin light was shining directly into my eyes. I heard a gun being cocked. My stomach turned over in fear.

12   Then I heard a surprised gasp. "You're just a kid!"

4 This passage is written from what point of view?

   A first person, told by a girl in Normandy

   B first person, told by the downed pilot

   C third person, told by an outside observer

   D third person, told by a girl in Normandy

5 Explain how the point of view adds suspense to the story. (3 points)

_____

_____

_____

_____

6 Which of the following details supports the theme that kids can be heroes?

   A *A sharp, bright moon had come out from behind the clouds.*

   B *. . . I had one advantage. I had played in these woods for years. I knew every inch of the ground by heart.*

   C *A pencil-thin light was shining directly into my eyes. I heard a gun being cocked.*

   D *Maybe the Nazis didn't know the downed pilot had bailed out, but it was more likely that they did.*

7 Explain how paragraph 6 develops the setting of the story. (3 points)

_____

_____

_____

Test-Taking Tips

1 Figurative language is not literally true. Think about the image the writer is trying to communicate.

2 Words may have similar meanings (denotations), but different emotional associations (connotations). To understand the connotation of a word, ask yourself if the word gives you positive or negative feelings.

3 To describe the mood of a story or poem, think about how the author's words make you feel. Make sure you can support your choice of mood with words or phrases from the text.

4 To figure out the point of view of a passage, look for pronouns. If you see *I*, *me*, and *we*, the story is in first-person point of view. If you see the pronouns *he*, *she*, *they*, and *them*, the story is in third-person point of view.

Go for it!

Unit Two Practice Test

Estimated time: 18 minutes

Directions: Read the following passage. Then answer the questions that follow.

Arrival

Kimo looked out the window of the plane. The sky was so blue it almost hurt his eyes. In San Carlo, it was usually smoggy. Below him lay the island of Oahu.

Kimo stared at the endless ocean. The edges of the water hugged the wide beaches. Wave after wave rolled onto the shore.

Kimo saw high, cloud-wrapped mountains. How mysterious they looked! At their feet lay a city, its towers reaching toward the sky.

Whump! Whump! He heard the landing gear come down. His heart raced. He would be glad to be down on the ground again after flying over water for five hours.

Then, the sound of the engines in reverse roared through the plane. Kimo gripped the arms of his seat. The whole plane trembled like the ground during an earthquake. When he looked around, though, no one else seemed worried. The passenger sitting to his left did not bat an eyelid.

Kimo looked anxiously out the window. The plane began to slow down, and, finally, it came to a stop. Kimo realized he was sweating. Whew! He didn't need any more adventures. This was plenty.

Now that he was no longer scared, he felt a little blue. Maybe he was homesick already. Frowning, Kimo grabbed his bag from the overhead bin.

"Aloha," the flight attendant said, smiling. He walked through the exit door. A wave of heat met him. Even the air smelled different.

---

1 Explain the meaning of the line "The edges of the water hugged the wide beaches." Does the word hugged have a positive or negative connotation? (3 points)

_____

_____

_____

2 The "whole plane trembled like the ground during an earthquake" means that—

   A there was an earthquake on the land below them.

   B the plane came to a very sudden stop.

   C the shaking felt as though it came from deep underground.

   D the plane felt as if it were being shaken.

3 The passage is written from what point of view?

   A in first person from Kimo's point of view

   B in third person from Kimo's point of view

   C in first person from an outside narrator's point of view

   D in third person from an outside narrator's point of view

4 The author uses the point of view in this story to—

   A build suspense about whether the plane will crash.

   B show a contrast between Kimo's attitude and the beautiful scenery.

   C explain the perspective of several of the characters in the story.

   D understand why Kimo is coming to Oahu.

5 Based on the context, what does the word <u>smoggy</u> mean?

   A clear

   B blue

   C cloudy

   D bright

6 Reread the following line from the passage.

The whole plane trembled like the ground during an earthquake.

Comparing the plane landing to an earthquake adds to Kimo's mood of—

   A fear.

   B peace.

   C mystery.

   D calm.

7 Which of the following lines BEST explains the setting of the story?

   A *Kimo looked out the window of the plane.*

   B *Below him lay the island of Oahu.*

   C *The passenger sitting to his left did not bat an eyelid.*

   D *He didn't need any more adventures. This was plenty.*

8 How do the final two paragraphs help you understand the conflict Kimo is facing in the story? Support your conclusions with evidence from the passage. (3 points)

_____

_____

_____

_____

_____

STOP

Points Earned/Total = _____ /12

Reading Literature
Lesson 6

Comparing and Contrasting Literature

Review the Standards (RL.6.9, W.6.8, W.6.9)

- **Compare** and **contrast** texts in different forms or **genres**
- Gather information from multiple print sources
- Draw **evidence** from literary texts

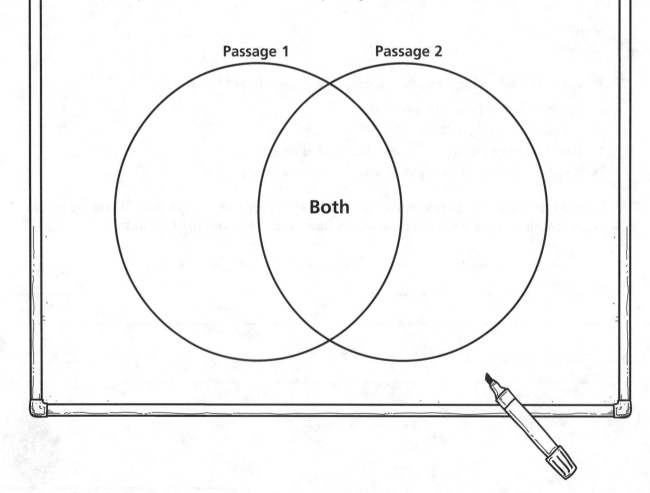

Q: How do I **compare** and **contrast** texts?

A: Comparing is showing how two texts are the same; **contrasting** is showing how two texts are different. Often two texts are about the same topic but are different genres, or types, of literature. A Venn diagram can help you compare and contrast the genre, characters, mood, and themes of two pieces. As always, you should support your comparison of two texts by using **evidence** from the text.

Passage 1   Passage 2

Both

Directions: Read the following passages. Then answer the questions that follow.

The following passage is an excerpt from a novel about two boys from the city who are hiking in a national park. The boys have climbed some boulders to look around and have a snack.

from Danger Canyon
by Margo Sorenson

Calvin stopped chewing. "What was that?" he asked, his mouth full. "That noise. Did you just open a bag or something?"

Rob set his soda down. He looked puzzled. "No, why?" he asked.

"It sounded like a bag of chips opening or something," Calvin said. "You sure?" he asked again. His heart began to pump.

"I don't even *have* any chips," Rob said slowly.

"Then what made that crackling sound?" Calvin whispered. Did he dare look over the side of the boulder?

Crackle! There it was again. Something was down there . . .

Calvin's heart raced. What was down there? He looked at Rob. Rob's face was white. His eyes were wide with fright. What should they do?

Calvin lay down on his stomach. He inched his way across the boulder. He tried to keep his belt buckle from scraping on the granite. He held his breath. He was almost to the edge. He waited and listened. Nothing. All he heard were the pines.

Calvin took a deep breath. *All right*, he told himself. *This is it*. He eased his head slowly over the edge of the huge boulder.

Suddenly, a streak of yellow flashed below. It raced back into the forest.

"Holy cow!" Calvin yelled. He sat up. "It was a mountain lion! I saw it!"

Rob scrambled over. He looked in the direction Calvin was looking.

"Are you sure?" Rob asked. "I don't see anything." He peered into the forest.

Calvin strained his eyes. It was hard to tell what was a shadow of a tree and what might be something else. "I know it!" he cried. "It was yellow! And could it move! It was fast!"

Rob looked doubtful. "Are you sure it wasn't a big chipmunk?" he asked. "A squirrel? A deer? Or maybe someone's dog? Mountain lions don't like to get close to people, do they?"

"I swear it looked like one," Calvin said. But then he stopped. He hadn't actually gotten a good look at it. All he had seen was a yellow flash. "Maybe you're right," Calvin admitted. "I am kind of jumpy today."

Mountain Lion

Mountain lion, why are you feared
For living life in your own way?
A tawny ghost, aloof and alone—
You silently search for prey.

Your ropelike tail's a blur in the dusk
As it brushes the earth behind you.
Mountain lion, why are you feared
For simply doing what you must do?

©Corel

1 "Danger Canyon" is an example of which genre?

   A poetry
   B drama
   C fiction
   D nonfiction

2 "Mountain Lion" is an example of which genre?

   A poetry
   B drama
   C short story
   D nonfiction

3 How are the mountain lions in the two passages similar?

   A They are both wild and unpredictable.
   B They both cause people to be afraid.
   C They are both friendly and easy to see.
   D They both need to be protected from humans.

Examples 1 and **2** ask you to identify the **genre**, or the type of literature, of each passage. "Danger Canyon" tells the fictional story of two boys who think they see a mountain lion. For **Example 1**, the correct answer is **choice C**.

For **Example 2**, the best choice is **A** because the passage contains elements of **poetry** such as rhyme and stanzas.

Example 3 asks you to think about how the two passages are similar. In other words, you must **compare** the two passages. Since the topic of both passages is about mountain lions, it would be important to consider how mountain lions are described. Go back to the passages and look for evidence. In "Danger Canyon" we find "Rob's face was white. His eyes were wide with fright." The mountain lion is described as "a streak of yellow" that moves fast. In the second passage, the mountain lion is described as "A tawny ghost, aloof and alone." The question is asked, "why are you feared?" Based on these details, the best answer is **choice B**.

4 Contrast the two passages by explaining three ways the passages are different. Give relevant evidence to support how the pieces are different in genre, mood, and their approach to the topic. (5 points)

_____

_____

_____

_____

_____

_____

_____

_____

_____

_____

_____

_____

Test-Taking Tips

1 Underline important sections in the passages as you read them. Think about how they are alike or different in characterization, genre, theme, and author's style.

2 Before answering any questions in which you must write, make sure you understand what the question is asking. Underline important words. Always support your conclusions with details or direct quotations from the text.

Go for it!

Unit Three Practice Test

Estimated time: 18 minutes

Directions: Read the selections. Then answer the questions that follow.

Movie at the Multiplex

Jenny dashed from the van to her front porch as Grandma Eileen wheeled herself up the driveway. It was probably 90 degrees in the shade, and she wiped sweat from her forehead.

"Ahh," Jenny said, closing the front door behind Grandma Eileen. "Thank goodness for air-conditioned houses."

"And air-conditioned movie theaters," Grandma Eileen said, laughing.

"That movie was amazing," Jenny said. "The special effects were extremely cool! I nearly jumped out of my seat when the alien cruiser attacked the space station."

"It certainly was . . . lively," Grandma Eileen said. "But that theater had so many levels . . . with elevators, escalators, and doors every which way. I thought I would get lost going to buy popcorn by myself."

"Yeah, the multiplex is huge," Jenny said. "I bet it's one of the biggest movie-theater complexes ever built."

"Excuse me a minute," Grandma Eileen said, and she wheeled herself away to her bedroom. Returning, she held an old photo album in her lap. She opened it to a picture of a young man and woman standing in front of a large old theater decorated in gold trim. The girl's hair was blowing in her face, and the young man had his hand on his head holding down his derby hat. They were both laughing.

"That's me and your Grandpa Dan."

Dear Diary,

Today was a great day. I finally got to see Boris Karloff in Bride of Frankenstein. The show was great, although Grandma Marilyn says that the old silent movies she used to watch as a kid were better. She goes on and on about how Douglas Fairbanks Jr. was the best actor ever and how actors used to communicate with their eyes instead of spelling everything out. She says that back then a movie was only 10 cents, and she can't believe that it now costs 35 cents for a movie that includes popcorn and a soda. Old people always think things were better in the "good old days."

I met Dan, Joan, and Phillip at the Paramount Theater on Main Street. We had to wait in a long line to get tickets. While we were waiting, Phillip took our picture with his new camera. It was windy and my hair was blowing in my face. Dan's hat almost blew away twice before Phillip snapped the picture. Phillip says that I can have the picture after it's developed.

Eileen

---

1 In the selections you read, which characters would agree that the past is sometimes more interesting than the present?

A Jenny and Eileen

B Jenny and Grandma Marilyn

C Grandma Eileen and Grandma Marilyn

D Grandma Eileen and Dan

2 From the information in these two selections, Jenny and Eileen could BOTH be described as—

A shy.

B fun-loving.

C argumentative.

D regretful.

3 Which sentence BEST describes the theme of BOTH selections?

A Young people embrace new things while older people treasure the past.

B Young people do not understand how much better old-fashioned movies were.

C Older people do not want to understand what young people enjoy.

D Older people forget what it was like to be young.

4 Compare and contrast the genres, themes, and characters of the passages. Explain your answer using specific details from the selections. (5 points)

_____

_____

_____

_____

_____

_____

_____

_____

_____

_____

STOP

Points Earned/Total = _____ /8

Analysis and Inference

Review the Standards (RI.6.1, RH.6.1, RST.6.1)

- Give **evidence** to support **analysis**
- Make an **inference**

Q: How do I **analyze** nonfiction text?

A: Analysis means breaking big ideas into smaller ones. Breaking longer chapters of information into smaller facts helps you understand what you are reading. Your analysis of the text must be based upon **evidence** such as facts and details found in the text.

Q: How do I make an **inference**?

A: When you make an **inference**, you are drawing a conclusion based upon the text and what you already know. Sometimes the text will confirm your inference, but other times you will have to go to a different text.

 Try It

Directions: Read the following passage. Then answer the questions that follow.

The *Tomatina* of Buñol

1   Throwing food at others is generally frowned upon. That's not the case in the Spanish town of Buñol, however. Each August, 30,000 people gather there for the world's largest food fight. The *Tomatina* festival gets its name from the sole ammunition in the event, the tomato. Exactly how the festival began is unclear, but it was first celebrated in about 1945. Each year it has attracted more participants.

2   To prepare for the event, many residents cover their homes and businesses with plastic. On the day of the *Tomatina,* thousands gather in the town square to await the arrival of trucks bearing more than 275,000 pounds of ripe tomatoes. As the hour of the *Tomatina* nears, crowds begin chanting, "Tomatoes! Tomatoes! Tomatoes!"

3   At about noon a rocket is fired to start the event. On cue, trucks dump out the tomatoes. For exactly one hour, the plump red missiles go flying. Soon the streets, buildings, and people of Buñol are covered with seeds, juice, and pulp. Official rules dictate that before hurling tomatoes, throwers must crush them or puncture their skins. Some people wear goggles or protective clothing. Ironically, however, this can make them more inviting targets for fellow tomato tossers.

4   Once the fight is over, the participants head for special public showers. Huge hoses spray off buildings, streets, and people. By evening, the town is back to normal.

1   What fact from the text supports the idea that only tomatoes are permitted to be thrown during the festival?

   A Throwing food at others is generally frowned upon except in the Spanish town of Buñol.

   B It is unclear how the festival began.

   C On cue, trucks dump out more than 275,000 pounds of tomatoes.

   D The *Tomatina* festival gets its name from the sole ammunition in the event, the tomato.

2   We can infer that the residents of Buñol cover their homes and businesses with heavy plastic in order to—

   A decorate them for the festival.

   B catch the tomato juice for later use.

   C protect them from the flying tomatoes.

   D signal to visitors to leave them alone.

3   What evidence is there that the town of Buñol wholeheartedly embraces the *Tomatina* festival? Support your analysis using evidence from the text. (3 points)

   _____

   _____

   _____

   _____

To answer **Example 1**, you must decide which fact from the text supports the idea that only tomatoes are thrown during the festival. As you review each answer choice, you should think about which one supports this idea. **Choice D** explains that the "sole ammunition" is the tomato, so it is correct.

Example 2 asks you to make an **inference** about why residents cover their homes and businesses with plastic. You read in the text that tomatoes are thrown during the festival. Combine this fact with what you know about the mess tomatoes make when they break apart. We can infer that people would want to protect homes and buildings from the mess. Thus, the correct answer is **choice C**.

For **Example 3**, you must base your **analysis** upon evidence found in the text. Reread the text and underline details that support your ideas. Be sure to use these details in your answer. A good answer might look something like this:

Good: *The* Tomatina *festival appears to be fully supported by the town of Buñol because the event is very organized. The town arranges for trucks to drop 275,000 pounds of tomatoes in the town square. There are official rules about crushing or puncturing the tomatoes before throwing them. The town also erects public showers for festivalgoers to use to clean up when they are done. This is not a random food fight, but a well-organized event.*

A poor answer would use the text incorrectly or try to support the analysis using personal opinions rather than facts from the text.

Poor: *The* Tomatina *festival appears to be fully supported by the town of Buñol. Only tomatoes can be thrown. Everyone meets in the town square and shouts "Tomatoes! Tomatoes!" before the food fighting begins. I think it would be a lot of fun to throw tomatoes at people. I want to go to the* Tomatina *sometime.*

◎ Try It On Your Own

4   Why do you think participants must crush or puncture the tomatoes before they throw them? (2 points)

_____

_____

5   Explain the rules of the *Tomatina* festival based upon the text. (3 points)

_____

_____

_____

_____

Main Ideas and Supporting Details

Review the Standards
(RI.6.2, RH.6.2, RST.6.2, RI.6.3, RH.6.3)

- Determine a **central idea** and supporting **details**
- Provide a **summary**
- Analyze how information is **introduced** and **elaborated**

Q: How do I write a **summary**?

A: To write a **summary**, you must first find the central idea of a text. The first sentence of your summary should explain the main idea. The rest of your summary should contain important supporting **details**.

Q: How is information **introduced** and **elaborated** in a text?

A: A writer **introduces** and **elaborates**, or gives details about, the main idea through illustrations, examples, definitions, and **anecdotes**, or stories. For example, in a historical text, a writer might introduce a famous person by telling an anecdote about him or her.

 Try It

Read the following passage. Then answer the questions that follow.

Stalactites and Stalagmites

In caves, mineral deposits form hauntingly beautiful structures called *stalactites* and *stalagmites*. Stalactites are shaped like icicles, and they hang from ceilings in caves. They form when moisture collects and drips, then evaporates and leaves crystallized minerals behind. Over time, these minerals build upon one another, forming a stalactite.

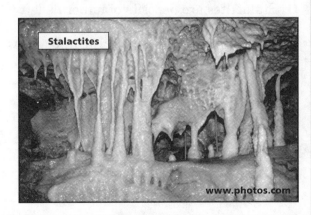

Stalactites

www.photos.com

Stalagmites are similar to stalactites, but they build upward from the cave floor. They form when water drips to the floor. As the moisture evaporates, the mineral deposits left behind slowly build up into a cone shape. Sometimes stalagmites and stalactites meet and form a column that stretches from floor to ceiling.

It has taken millions of years for some of the world's most spectacular cave formations to form. However, these natural wonders are fragile and can be damaged if touched. Even air pollution is bad for cave formations. Naturalists in places like New Mexico's Carlsbad Caverns are working hard to preserve stalactites and stalagmites while still making them accessible to visitors.

www.photos.com
Stalagmites

1 What is the central idea of this passage?

  A Stalagmites are similar to stalactites.

  B Stalactites and stalagmites are natural wonders formed by mineral deposits.

  C You can see stalactites and stalagmites in many places.

  D As moisture evaporates, mineral deposits are left behind.

2 Which of the following details would BEST support the main idea of the first paragraph?

  A Stalactites usually grow anywhere between a quarter-inch and an inch every century.

  B Stalagmites look like traffic cones on the floor of a cave.

  C Bats often hang from the ceilings of underground caves.

  D You can grow your own stalactites and stalagmites using common household items.

3 The pictures illustrate which of the following points?

  A It takes millions of years for cave formations to form.

  B Sometimes stalagmites and stalactites meet to form a column.

  C Air pollution is bad for cave formations.

  D Stalactites are deposits of minerals left when moisture evaporates.

4 Write a summary of the passage. (3 points)

_____

_____

_____

_____

_____

_____

Example 1 asks you to think about the **central idea** of the passage. As you read through the answer choices, think about which one gives a broad overview of the entire passage. You can eliminate choice D because it gives a detail about how stalagmites and stalactites are formed. Choice A is the main idea of the second paragraph, but not the entire passage. The best answer is **choice B**.

For **Example 2**, you must think about the main idea of the first paragraph. As you reread the paragraph, you understand that the central idea is about stalactites. The only answer that contains a supporting detail about stalactites is **choice A**.

To answer **Example 3**, you must think about how the pictures illustrate the ideas you read in the passage. As you read through the answer choices, it is clear that the pictures show how stalagmites and stalactites can meet to form a column, or **choice B**.

Example 4 asks you to write a **summary**. A summary should contain the main idea and any important supporting details. When writing a summary of an entire passage, include the central idea of the passage and then the main ideas from each of the supporting paragraphs. It may be helpful to reread the passage and underline the topic sentence of each paragraph.

Good: *Stalactites and stalagmites are mineral formations found in caves. Stalactites form on the ceiling of caves as moisture drips down and then evaporates, leaving crystallized minerals behind. Stalagmites are similar, but they build upward from the floor of the cave. Cave formations are very fragile, so steps are being taken to preserve them for years to come.*

A poor summary doesn't include the main idea of the passage or contains unimportant or incorrect details.

Poor: *Stalactites and stalagmites are found in caves. One forms from the ceiling of the cave and the other from the floor. Sometimes they join, forming one long column from floor to ceiling. New Mexico's Carlsbad Caverns is closed to visitors.*

 **Try It On Your Own**

Directions: Read the passage and answer the questions that follow.

The California Gold Rush

The desire for gold dates far back in the history of humankind, and the discovery of this valuable metal has always caused adventurous people to rush to the spot where someone has first seen it.

The discovery of gold in California has been important to its history. In 1848 a man by the name of James Sutter was building a sawmill in California. James Marshall, who was helping him, noticed some flakes of yellow metal mixed in with the gravel from the stream. Tests showed these flakes to be gold, and the California gold rush was on.

It was called the Gold Rush of '49. Men and women who came to California to search for gold were called "the forty-niners." A few found gold and grew rich; others died from the heat or starved or turned back before even reaching California. Others failed to find gold but stayed in California and found other jobs. It was this large number of settlers coming to California who changed the history of the region.

5 Which of the following BEST explains the central idea of the passage?

   A A man named James Sutter was building a sawmill in California.

   B The desire for gold dates far back in the history of humankind.

   C James Marshall was the first man to find flakes of gold in a stream.

   D The California Gold Rush of '49 is an important historical event.

6 The first paragraph introduces the central idea by—

   A giving examples of other gold rushes.

   B telling a story about a gold miner.

   C describing the causes of gold rushes.

   D explaining how California became a state.

7 Which of the following details supports the idea that the Gold Rush was important to the history of California?

   A Gold was discovered in 1848.

   B Very few people actually found gold and grew rich.

   C A large number of settlers changed the history of the region.

   D The men and women who came to find gold were called the "forty-niners."

8 Write a summary of the passage. (3 points)

_____

_____

_____

_____

Test-Taking Tips

1 When asked about supporting details in a passage, think carefully before you select an answer. Often, more than one answer choice may seem correct. Choose the answer that gives specific information about the main idea of the passage.

2 Summaries should state the main idea and most important details as briefly as possible. Be concise!

3 Summaries should not contain your personal opinions about the text.

Go for it!

Unit Four Practice Test

Estimated time: 18 minutes

Directions: Read the passage and the graphic organizer. Then answer the questions that follow.

Natural Disasters:
Tornadoes and Hurricanes

1   Tornadoes and hurricanes both produce some of nature's most frightening winds. But why is one so much harder to predict than the other? Tornadoes often form with little warning. After a destructive journey across land, they can die down only minutes after forming. Hurricanes, however, form slowly, can last for weeks, and cover a much larger area. Forecasters have much less time to warn people about tornadoes.

2   Tornadoes form when warm air rises into a thunderstorm. As that air rises, more air rushes in to take its place. This causes the thunderstorm to draw in and feed off the warm, wet air. The rising air collides with other winds, and together they twist together like a rope. In a matter of minutes, the wind speed of these funnel clouds can reach over 300 mph!

3   One of the scariest things about a tornado is that you never know exactly where, when, or if it's going to happen. Forecasters can tell ahead of time if a tornado *might* happen. They can even determine the approximate time of day when it might happen. But until it does happen, they never know for sure. When a tornado actually forms, the people in its path might have only minutes to take shelter.

4   Hurricanes, however, give forecasters much more warning. A hurricane starts as a thunderstorm near the equator. As warm ocean waters feed the storm, the winds begin to swirl at high speeds. With winds up to 38 mph, this storm is called a *tropical depression*.

5   As the storm keeps gathering strength, the winds grow stronger. When they reach 39 mph, it becomes a tropical storm. The storm officially becomes a hurricane when the winds reach a speed of 74 mph or more.

6   Forecasters can watch storms turn into hurricanes for a week or more. As they watch the storm grow, forecasters predict where the hurricane will hit land several days ahead of its arrival. When the storm is 8 to 16 hours away, warnings are put out and an evacuation is advised or ordered.

©DigitalStock

©DigitalStock

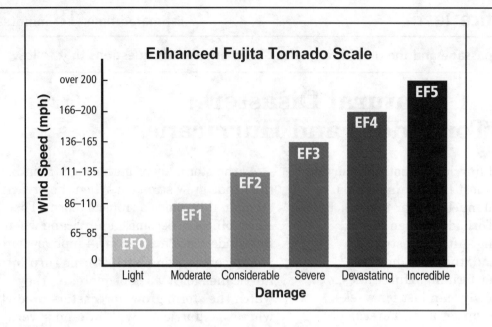

Enhanced Fujita Tornado Scale

1   The first paragraph introduces the topic of the passage by—

A showing how tornadoes and hurricanes are different.

B detailing how tornadoes and hurricanes are formed.

C defining both tornadoes and hurricanes.

D giving examples of historic tornadoes and hurricanes.

2   From the passage we can infer that—

A hurricane winds do not reach 300 mph.

B more people are killed by hurricanes than by tornadoes.

C more tornadoes than hurricanes occur every year.

D forecasters are better at warning people about hurricanes than tornadoes.

3   Which of the following is the central idea of the passage?

A Hurricanes and tornadoes both produce high, damaging winds.

B Tornadoes form over land, but hurricanes form over the ocean.

C Forecasters can predict when a tornado might happen, but they never know for sure.

D While both hurricanes and tornadoes are dangerous windstorms, tornadoes are more difficult to predict.

4   In the body of the passage, the information on tornadoes and hurricanes is developed by—

A explaining how the storms are formed and how difficult they are to predict.

B telling anecdotes about the deadliest storms in the past 50 years.

C explaining how forecasters predict each type of storm.

D giving facts about how to protect yourself from violent windstorms.

5 The graphic organizer elaborates which idea found in the passage?

   A Tornadoes form with little warning.

   B Forecasters can even determine the approximate time of day when a tornado will happen.

   C Tornadoes die down only minutes after forming.

   D The wind speed of tornadoes can reach over 300 mph.

6 Write a summary of the passage. (3 points)

_____

_____

_____

_____

_____

_____

_____

_____

_____

_____

_____

_____

Points Earned/Total = _____ /8

Word Meanings

Review the Standards (RI.6.4, RH.6.4, RST.6.4, L.6.4.a)
• Determine the meaning of words and phrases
• Use **context** as a clue to the meaning of a word or phrase

Q: How do I determine the meaning of words and phrases in a nonfiction text?

A: First, try using context clues, or the other words in the sentence. The following chart explains types of context clues.

Type of Context Clue	How It Provides a Clue	Example
Definition	explains the meaning	A <u>feline</u> is *an animal belonging to the cat family.*
Example	illustrates or gives a sample	Bobcats sometimes attack small <u>livestock</u>, *such as pigs, chickens, and sheep.*
Restatement	states definition of word again using a different word or phrase	Pumas live in <u>remote</u> areas of the park. Few people travel to these *distant* areas.
Contrast	uses an opposite	Most park animals are *active during the day.* Mountain cats, however, are <u>nocturnal</u>.

Second, think about any technical meaning the word may have in the passage. Consider the word *bill*. In everyday life, your parents must pay bills, or a statement of money owed to someone. However, when you read in your social studies book that the Senate passed a bill about health care, the word *bill* takes on a technical meaning related to government. In this case a *bill* is a proposal for a new law. Definitions for technical words are often provided in a glossary at the end of the book or in a box or sidebar within the chapter.

Read the following passage and answer the questions that follow.

Caught on Camera: The Mysterious Giant Squid

1   The image of a giant squid lurking in the deep sea may seem like a scene from a horror movie. However, these enormous creatures are very real. Whalers have spotted them battling whales, fishermen have found them in their nets, and their bodies have washed onto ocean beaches. But until recently, no one had ever seen a live giant squid up close in its deep ocean <u>habitat</u>.

2   In September 2004, a group of Japanese <u>marine biologists</u> became the first to view and photograph a living giant squid in its natural habitat. Three thousand feet deep in the North Pacific Ocean, the scientists used bait to attract the squid. They hooked shrimp onto the end of a fishing line and waited. When the giant squid approached the shrimp, the scientists began clicking away. They were able to take over 500 images. The photos show the squid devouring the bait and struggling to free itself from the fishing hook.

3   Giant squids sometimes grow to 60 feet—possibly longer. Their eight arms and two tentacles are covered with suckers. The long <u>tentacles</u>, used for feeding, have spoon-like clubs at their ends.

4   Squids move by squirting water through a funnel near their heads. The fins on their tube-shaped bodies help them <u>maneuver</u>. When fleeing an enemy, they sometimes squirt a dark, inky liquid into the water. This allows the squid to hide itself and confuse its <u>adversary</u>.

5   Thanks to the new photos, scientists are learning even more about how giant squids move. For example, they once thought that giant squids could not move very quickly. They now know that they are capable of strong and rapid movements and that they chase their prey very energetically.

1   The best definition for the word <u>habitat</u> in paragraph 1 is—

   A "a special underwater camera."

   B "a dark underwater cave."

   C "an environment where an animal normally lives."

   D "a submarine used by biologists to study life underwater."

2   Based on context clues, define the term <u>tentacles</u>. (3 points)

_____

_____

_____

Example 1 asks you to define the word *habitat*. The phrase *But until recently* indicates a contrast between where squids have been found (in fishermen's nets, battling whales, on beaches) and where they normally live in the deep ocean. We can conclude that habitat means a place where an animal usually lives, or **choice C**.

For **Example 2**, you must write a definition of the word *tentacles*. From the **context clues** you know that tentacles are similar to arms, but longer and covered with suckers. These suckers must help them capture and hold their prey so they can eat. A good definition might look like this:

Good: *Tentacles are long, armlike body parts covered with suckers and used by squids to hold and eat their food.*

A poor example will incorrectly define the word or be incomplete.

Poor: *Tentacles are fins used by squid.*

◎ Try It On Your Own

3 A marine biologist is a—

   A fisherman who catches squid.

   B scientist who studies sea creatures.

   C person who enjoys the sea.

   D sailor.

4 Based upon the context, define the word maneuver. (3 points)

   _____

   _____

   _____

5 A word meaning the opposite of adversary is—

   A friend.

   B prey.

   C predator.

   D fish.

Reading Informational Text Lesson 10

Text Structures and Purpose

Review the Standards
(RI.6.5, RH.6.5, RST.6.5, RI.6.6, RH.6.6, RST.6.6)

- Analyze how a section of a text fits into the overall **structure** and ideas
- Determine an author's **point of view** or **purpose**

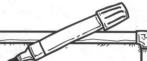

Q: How do I analyze the **structure** of a text?

A: You analyze a text **structure** by identifying how content is organized. Analyzing text structures will help you understand what you are reading. The following chart explains some common text structures.

Organizational Structure	Description
Logical Order	Facts are presented so that each idea builds upon the ideas that precede it.
Chronological Order	Events are presented in the order that they occur.
Cause and Effect	The text explains what happens and why it happens.
Compare and Contrast	The text tells how two or more things are the same and different.
Classification	Ideas are grouped according to common characteristics.

Q: How do I figure out an author's **point of view** or **purpose** for writing a passage?

A: Think about why the author is writing. Common **purposes** are listed on the chart below.

Author's Purpose	Description
To Persuade	The author tries to convince the reader to think or believe in a certain way.
To Inform	The author provides readers with factual information about a topic.
To Instruct or Explain	The author explains to readers how to do something or achieve a goal.
To Entertain	The author relates an interesting, suspenseful, or amusing story about a real or imaginary event.

A writer's point of view is her opinion about the facts she is presenting. Look for statements with words like *good, bad, must,* and *should*.

GO ON

Directions: Read the following passage. Then answer the questions that follow.

The Life Cycle of the Sun

1   For more than four and a half billion years, the Sun has provided heat and light to the planets in our solar system. This energy is produced by a process called *nuclear fusion*. In this process, hydrogen is converted to helium in the Sun's core. Scientists predict that the Sun has enough hydrogen left to keep it shining as it is for another five billion years.

The Life Cycle of a Star

2   All living things go through a life cycle that includes birth, growth, and finally death. Stars have their own kind of life cycle. All stars in the universe follow a life cycle determined by their size. Large stars form quickly and have short lives, while small, low-mass stars have vast life spans. Astronomers have classified the Sun as a young, average-sized, yellow star. Because the Sun is an average-sized star, it will probably progress from its current state through several stages. First it will become a red giant, then a white dwarf, and finally, a black dwarf.

Our Sun's Future

3   Scientists estimate that in about five billion years, the Sun's center will begin to shrink and heat up. The higher core temperature will cause hydrogen to be converted to helium more rapidly, thus producing more energy. As a result, the outer regions of the Sun will expand and turn reddish in color. The Sun will have become a red giant.

4   After the Sun has used up its energy as a red giant, it will begin to shrink. Once it has shrunk to the size of the Earth, it will enter its white dwarf phase. As a white dwarf, it will continue to lose heat.

5   Billions of years later, the Sun will enter its final, black dwarf stage. At the end of its life, it will no longer give off heat and light. It will lie motionless, and the planets in our solar system will grow cold and dark. The life cycle of our Sun will be over.

1   The author's purpose for writing this passage is to—

A   persuade the reader that the Sun is not a planet but a star.

B   inform the reader about the life cycle of the Sun.

C   instruct the reader on how to determine which cycle a star is in.

D   entertain readers with a scary story about how the Sun is going to burn out.

2 What organizational structure is used in paragraph 2?

   A compare and contrast

   B chronological order

   C cause and effect

   D classification

3 How will the shrinking and heating up of the Sun's center result in more energy being produced?

   A It will produce more energy by speeding up the conversion of hydrogen to helium.

   B It will cause the outer regions of the Sun to expand.

   C It will result in the Sun's surface turning red in color.

   D It will result in a higher core temperature.

4 Paragraph 4 serves as a transition between which pair of ideas?

   A the Sun becoming a red giant and the Sun dying

   B the Sun becoming a red giant and its center shrinking

   C the Sun using up its energy and the Sun becoming a red giant

   D the Sun becoming a black dwarf and the Sun dying

5 Explain how the section **The Life Cycle of a Star** fits into the overall purpose of the passage. Support your conclusions with details from the text. (3 points)

_____

_____

_____

_____

_____

Example 1 asks you to think about the author's **purpose** for writing. Think about the main ideas presented in the text based upon what you read, the title, and the section headings. These all point to the answer, which is **choice B**.

Example 2 asks you to identify the organizational structure of a specific paragraph in the passage. In the second paragraph, the author explains the life cycle of a star. Life cycles occur in *chronological order*. **Choice B** is correct.

Example 3 asks you to identify an effect of the Sun's center shrinking and heating up. To answer this question, you must apply the organizational structure of a paragraph. Paragraph 3 explains what happens when the Sun's center begins to shrink and heat up. All four choices name effects found in the paragraph; however, only choice A is an effect that pertains to producing more energy. **Choice A** is correct.

Example 4 tests your understanding of another feature found in informational text—the *transition*. A transition is a word, phrase, sentence, or paragraph that connects ideas within a text. For example, in the sentence, *Because the Sun is an average-sized star, it will probably progress from its current state through several stages*, the word

GO ON →

because is a transition that connects the Sun's size to the stages that it will go through. For this question, you are asked to identify the ideas that are connected by paragraph 4, a transitional paragraph. The paragraph before paragraph 4 discusses the Sun becoming a red giant. The paragraph that follows paragraph 4 tells about the end of the Sun's life cycle. The only choice that includes both ideas is choice A, *the Sun becoming a red giant and the Sun dying*. **Choice A** is correct.

To answer **Example 5**, you must think about how one section of the passage contributes to the main idea. We know the purpose of the passage is to explain the cycle through which the Sun will proceed for the next five billion years. The section called The Life Cycle of a Star explains the general process that all stars go through in their lifetime. A good answer might look like this:

Good: *The section "The Life Cycle of a Star" explains that the Sun is a star and then gives the steps that stars go through in their life cycle. This contributes to the entire passage by defining the terms and describing the general process that will be explained in detail in the rest of the passage.*

◎ Try It On Your Own

Directions: Read the following passage, and then answer the questions that follow.

Coins

1 Most people don't give much thought to the common little objects that jangle around in their pockets. Coins, keys, perhaps a safety pin or two—they're just *there*, waiting to be used. But have you ever wondered how nickels, dimes, and quarters are made? Or who invented the key? And aren't you glad someone invented a pin that won't poke you? Each of these common metal objects has its own history and unique manufacturing process.

The First Coins

2 The first true coins were made in Turkey. They were produced from a mixture of melted gold and silver called *electrum*. One side was stamped with a picture of a lion. The other side had punch marks to show its weight and value.

3 Coins are still made from stamped metal today. Quarters, dimes, and nickels are silver-colored, but they're made from cupro-nickel, a mixture of copper and nickel. Pennies are made from copper and zinc.

Making U.S. Coins

4 To mint a coin, two designs are chosen—one for the front and one for the back. An artist turns each design into a big plaster model, or relief. Every detail must be perfect.

5 Small copies of each design are cut into steel dies. One die will imprint the coin's front, or head side. The other die will stamp the coin's back, or tail side.

6 The pattern on each die is the reverse of the original. But when the die stamps the coin, the design will be correct.

7 Sheets of metal are rolled to the right thickness. The sheets sometimes are a quarter-mile long!

8 A blanking machine cuts thousands of small disks from the metal sheets. The disks are called *blanks* because there is no design on them yet. They are the same size as the finished coins. A different machine makes the ridges around the edge. The leftover metal is melted again.

9 Blanks become coins during a process known as *striking*. The blanks are heated until they're soft. Then they are cleaned in acid. In the coining press, the metal dies stamp both sides of a blank at the same time.

10 The finished coins are inspected carefully. If the designs aren't clear or the coins are dented, they are remade.

Today quarters, dimes, and nickels are made from cupro-nickel, a mixture of copper and nickel.

www.photos.com

6 Which of the following BEST describes the author's main purpose for writing this passage?

A to entertain readers with an amusing story about what we keep in our pockets

B to persuade readers to check their pockets for coins

C to inform readers about the U.S. mint

D to explain the process of making coins

7 The text under the heading **Making U.S. Coins** is organized using what text structure?

A chronological order

B logical order

C cause and effect

D comparison and contrast

8 Which organizational structure is used in paragraph 3?

    A chronological order

    B logical order

    C cause and effect

    D comparison and contrast

9 Explain the author's purpose for writing the passage. Support your answer using evidence from the text. (3 points)

_____

_____

_____

_____

Test-Taking Tips

1 To help determine an author's purpose, think about the type of text you are reading and in what kind of publication it is likely to appear. Newspaper and magazine articles are usually written to inform. Manuals are written to explain. Advertisements try to persuade.

2 Context clues may not be in the same sentence as the word you are trying to define. Look for clues in the sentences before and after. Context clues include phrases that hint at the meaning of the word, such as *for example, such as,* and *unlike*.

3 When determining the text structure of a passage, look for word clues. To find causes and effects, look for signal words and phrases such as *because, as a result of,* and *since*. Passages that explain events in a sequence use words such as *before, first, then,* and *finally*.

Go for it!

Unit Five Practice Test

Estimated time: 18 minutes

Directions: Read the passage. Then answer the questions that follow.

©Corel

Madagascar's Leaping Lemurs

1   **I**f you were to visit the island of Madagascar off the southeast coast of Africa, you might witness something seen nowhere else in the world—a "lemur ballet." The jumping *sifaka* lemurs resemble dancers as they leap through the grass. In addition to leaping lemurs, many other kinds of lemurs also live on Madagascar.

2   Lemurs are members of the **primate** family, which makes them distant cousins of monkeys and apes. Like these primates, lemurs have five fingers on their hands. Because their thumbs and big toes are built for grasping, lemurs, monkeys, and apes can easily climb trees and hang from branches.

3   There are, however, some key differences between lemurs and other primates. Lemurs have moist, pointed noses. Monkeys have flatter faces and dry noses. Lemurs rely heavily on their strong sense of smell to recognize what they can eat and to distinguish members of a social group. Apes and monkeys depend more on their sense of vision. Lemurs also cannot use their fingers to groom each other like apes and monkeys can. They use their teeth! Almost all lemurs have long furry tails that help them balance when they leap through the trees. Unlike monkeys, lemurs cannot hang from their tails.

4   There are about 32 different types of lemurs on Madagascar today. They range in size from the *pygmy mouse* lemur, which weighs about one ounce, to the 28-inch, 15-pound *indri*. One of the more famous lemurs is the *ring-tailed* lemur. It has a gray back, white underparts, and rings of black and white fur on its tail. The slightly larger *ruffed* lemurs have a fluffy white ruff, or collar, of fur around their necks. The two largest lemurs, the indri and sifaka, have powerful hind legs,

which they use to spring from tree to tree. The sifakas cannot walk on all fours like other lemurs. When they are on the ground, they stand upright and leap sideways. This makes a group of them moving in unison look like dancers in a ballet. Perhaps the most unusual lemur is the *aye-aye*. It has a long, skinny middle finger that it uses to scoop insects out of hollow branches.

5   Lemurs are **arboreal** animals that can jump from branch to branch horizontally or vertically. When different species of lemurs live in the same area, they treat layers of the forest as if they were floors in a "lemur hotel." One kind of lemur might reside in the top of the forest. Another may use the mid-layer, while a third uses the forest floor. The ring-tailed lemur is the only lemur that spends most of its time on the ground.

6   The larger lemurs are active in the early morning or evening. Smaller lemurs are active mostly at night. Most lemurs eat fruit, leaves, flowers, and nectar. Like other primates, they may sometimes eat insects, eggs, and small birds. Smaller lemurs, such as the aye-aye, eat mostly insects.

7   Most lemurs are social, living in groups of 3 to 24. Male and female lemurs are generally the same size, and most groups are ruled by a dominant female who has first access to food. Social lemurs use complex calls and body postures to communicate. Calls signal their presence and ensure that other groups don't invade their territory. Lemurs also use calls to express their moods.

8   Ancestors of today's lemurs probably got to Madagascar by floating on a piece of vegetation, such as a tree branch. Over time, they evolved into about 50 different species of lemurs. Lemurs flourished on Madagascar because they didn't have competition from other primates.

9   Lemurs play an important role in their environment. They disperse seeds from the foods they eat, and this helps rejuvenate the forest. Lemurs also help feed ground-dwelling animals by shaking food loose from the trees as they move from branch to branch.

10   Although lemurs have few animal predators, humans pose a threat to them. Humans arrived on the island about 2000 years ago. By the time Europeans arrived on the island in the 1600s, 15 species of lemur were already extinct. The biggest threat lemurs face is habitat destruction. Farming, livestock grazing, and logging have destroyed 80 percent of the forest where lemurs live. Many people are now working to prevent more species from becoming extinct. Hopefully, future generations will be able to enjoy Madagascar's incredible lemur community.

1   Based upon the context of paragraph 5, where would you expect to find an *arboreal* animal?

   A on a mountaintop

   B in a forest

   C in a desert

   D in an underground tunnel

2 Using the context of paragraph 2, write a short definition of the term *primate*. (3 points)

_____

_____

_____

3 Which sentence serves as a transition between paragraph 2 and paragraph 3?

   A *Like these primates, lemurs have five fingers on their hands.*

   B *Because their thumbs and big toes are built for grasping, lemurs, monkeys, and apes can easily climb trees and hang from branches.*

   C *There are, however, some key differences between lemurs and other primates.*

   D *Lemurs have moist, pointed noses.*

4 What organizational structure is used in paragraph 3?

   A compare and contrast

   B logical order

   C cause and effect

   D classification

5 Reread the following sentence from the passage.

Lemurs are members of the primate family, which makes them distant cousins of monkeys and apes.

This sentence is an example of which type of organizational pattern?

   A compare and contrast

   B logical order

   C cause and effect

   D classification

6 Which of the following sentences reveals the author's point of view, or opinion, on saving lemurs from extinction?

   A *Although lemurs have few animal predators, humans pose a threat to them.*

   B *Farming, livestock grazing, and logging have destroyed 80 percent of the forest where lemurs live.*

   C *Many people are now working to prevent more species from becoming extinct.*

   D *Hopefully, future generations will be able to enjoy Madagascar's incredible lemur community.*

7 Which of the following paragraphs explains how lemurs arrived on Madagascar?

   A paragraph 1

   B paragraph 4

   C paragraph 8

   D paragraph 10

8 Explain the author's main purpose for writing this passage. Support your answer with evidence from the text. (3 points)

_____

_____

_____

_____

_____

_____

_____

_____

Points Earned/Total = _____/12

Unit Six—Integration of Knowledge and Ideas

Integrating Information

Review the Standards (RI.6.7, RH.6.7, RST.6.7, W.6.8)

- **Integrate** information from different formats and sources
- **Assess** the **credibility** of a source
- **Quote** or **paraphrase** while avoiding **plagiarism**

Q: What does **integrating** information from different formats mean?

A: Suppose you are doing a project on polar bears. You find some books from the library, and then you go online and find a Web site on polar bears. Not only will you find written information, but you will also find graphs on how the population of polar bears has declined and maps of where polar bears live. When you combine the information from the books and the Web site, you are **integrating** the information. Consider how some information is the same and some is different. If any facts are different, you may need to consult another source.

Q: How do I decide if information is **relevant**?

A: To decide if information is **relevant**, ask yourself the question, "Does this information fit with my purpose for writing?" If you are going to write about how the habitat of polar bears is declining due to climate change, you probably won't find appropriate information in an online article about the new polar bear exhibit at your local zoo. You would find relevant information on a Web site that documents the melting of the polar ice caps.

Q: How do I decide if a text is **credible**?

A: Credibility means the information is from a reliable source. A reliable text is written by an expert on the topic. A reliable source also tries to present the information fairly and doesn't have a hidden purpose, such as trying to get you to buy a product.

Q: What is the difference between **quoting** and **paraphrasing** information?

A: A quotation is taken word for word from a text and must be set off by quotation marks. **Paraphrasing** information means you put the information in your own words. Any time you use a direct quotation without quotation marks you are plagiarizing, or claiming someone else's writing is your own.

GO ON

Try It

Directions: Read the passage and study the Web site. Then answer the questions that follow.

Go Sola!

Sola is the excitement capital of the Pacific. With fun activities on both water and land, this island is a tropical paradise. Swim with colorful fish in warm seas. Explore miles of sparkling beaches. Hike through lush rain forests. Bike on rugged mountains. The island's natural wonders are endless.

Sola also offers opportunities for both recreation and leisure—from sailing to golf and restaurants to spas. And everything is priced to fit within your budget. During your vacation, you'll be relaxed, refreshed, and amazed. Come visit for the time of your life!

Travel and Lodging

Sola lies almost 3000 miles from the nearest land. However, most major airlines fly directly to our main airport. In addition, many cruise ships sail our waters.

Sola has many different types of lodging. Our resorts and spas are among the world's finest. Inns and small hotels offer privacy and solitude. For those desiring a "taste" of local culture, many residents rent their homes to visitors.

To explore Sola, most people rent a car. Motorcycles, scooters, and bicycles can be rented as well.

Things to Do on Sola

Use your imagination—if you can think of it, you can do it on Sola!

On the Water: You can kayak winding streams to remote areas. Or you can learn to surf the waves. Go sailing on one of the island's majestic yachts, or rent your own boat. Scuba diving, water skiing, deep-sea fishing, and snorkeling are also available.

In the Air: Helicopter tours give visitors a bird's-eye view of hidden valleys, thick jungles, and ancient lava flows.

On the Land: Sola's varied terrain challenges mountain bikers and four-wheel drivers alike. Horseback riding here is truly extraordinary. You can trot through forests or gallop through the surf. You may even want to help round up a herd of cattle on one of the island's three ranches.

Island Resources

Sola enjoys all the modern amenities, even though it is isolated in the middle of the Pacific. Every possible convenience is available. There are top-notch medical facilities. We have state-of-the-art communication, business, and financial services. If you're interested in buying property, simply visit one of our many real estate agents.

Weather

Sola's climate is mild and pleasant most of the year. However, it can get chilly at the higher elevations. If traveling there, bring long pants and several layers of clothing, as nighttime temperatures can drop into the 40s.

Sola's Climate

	J	F	M	A	M	J	J	A	S	O	N	D
Average Temperature	76°	77°	79°	80°	80°	82°	83°	84°	81°	80°	78°	77°
Average Rainfall	5"	5"	4"	4"	2"	3"	3"	4"	4"	7"	6"	5"

More Information

Come see what everyone's talking about! Book your vacation today. You can also visit our Web site at *www.gosola.com*. Once you've been to Sola, you'll never be the same!

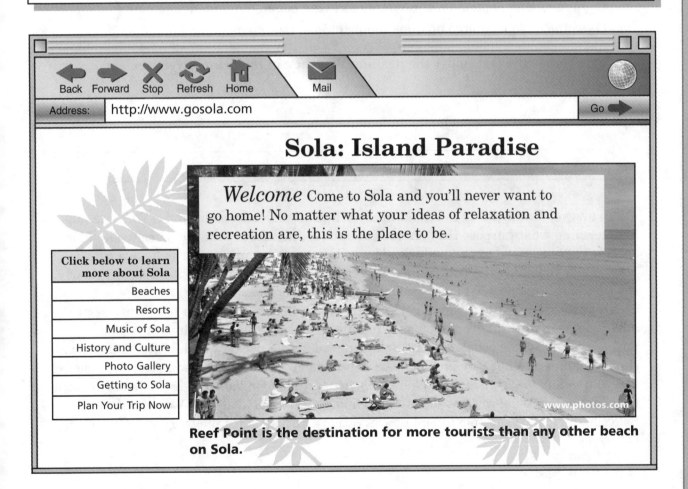

Back   Forward   Stop   Refresh   Home   Mail

Address: http://www.gosola.com   Go

Sola: Island Paradise

Welcome Come to Sola and you'll never want to go home! No matter what your ideas of relaxation and recreation are, this is the place to be.

Click below to learn more about Sola

Beaches

Resorts

Music of Sola

History and Culture

Photo Gallery

Getting to Sola

Plan Your Trip Now

www.photos.com

Reef Point is the destination for more tourists than any other beach on Sola.

GO ON

1 What is MOST likely the purpose of both the print advertisement and the Web site?

    A to describe the characteristics of tropical islands

    B to inform readers about the weather on Sola

    C to entertain readers with a story about the Pacific islands

    D to convince readers to visit Sola

2 BOTH the Web site and the print advertisement—

    A include information about the history of Sola.

    B use persuasive language.

    C allow people to make trip reservations.

    D offer photographs of scenes from Sola.

3 Where can you find out what Sola's most popular tourist beach is?

    A in the introductory paragraph of the print advertisement

    B in the print advertisement, under the heading "Things to Do on Sola"

    C in the photo caption on the Web site's home page

    D in the table that accompanies the print advertisement

4 Paraphrase the text under the heading **Weather** in the print advertisement. (3 points)

    _____

    _____

    _____

    To answer **Example 1**, you must analyze a print advertisement and a Web site page to determine what purpose they share. Functional and media materials are created for specific reasons, often to persuade readers to buy a certain product or believe a certain idea. When you study the text in the advertisement and on the Web site, you can clearly see that both urge people to visit Sola. **Choice D** is correct.

    To answer **Example 2**, you must **integrate** the information from the print advertisement with the Web site page. You already know that both have the same purpose—to convince people to visit Sola. Now you must decide which of the four answer choices names another way in which the two texts are the same. As you read each choice, ask yourself, _Is this true for the advertisement? Is it true for the Web site?_ The only choice for which you can answer yes to both questions is choice B. Only the Web site describes Sola's history, allows people to make reservations, and includes photographs. **Choice B** is correct.

Example 3 asks you to study the print advertisement and the Web site to determine where you can find the answer to a question. When you compare the information in the two selections, you can see that **choice C** is correct. Under the photograph on the Web site, the caption states that more tourists visit Reef Point than any other beach on Sola.

Example 4 asks you to paraphrase information from a section of the text. To do this you should reread the section and then rewrite it in your own words.

Good: *Sola has a very mild climate all year round. Temperatures range from the mid-70s to the mid-80s. If you plan to travel to the mountains, bring warmer clothes because at night the temperatures drop into the 40s. If you want to avoid the rainy season, don't go to Sola in October or November. May, June, and July bring the least amount of rainfall.*

Poor: *Sola's climate is mild and pleasant most of the year. However, it can get chilly. At the higher elevations, bring long pants, as nighttime temperatures can drop into the 40s.*

◎ Try It On Your Own

Use the passage and Web site on Sola to answer the following questions.

5   The information found in these sources would be most relevant if you were—

   A planning a vacation to Sola.

   B writing about the history of Sola.

   C comparing Sola's climate to Hawaii's climate.

   D researching islands in the Pacific.

6   Which of the following would be helpful if you wanted to know the best time of year to go mountain biking on Sola?

   A in the print advertisement, under "Travel and Lodging"

   B in the table in the print advertisement, under "Weather"

   C on the Web site, under "Photo Gallery"

   D on the Web site, under "Getting to Sola"

7   Is the information from the passage and the Web site credible? Would it be appropriate if you wanted to get a well-rounded view of life on Sola? Use direct quotations from the passage to support your answer. (3 points)

   _____

   _____

   _____

   _____

Evaluating Arguments

Review the Standards (RI.6.8, RH.6.8, RST.6.8)

- Trace and evaluate the **argument** and **claims** in a text
- Identify claims that are supported by **reasons** and **evidence**
- Identify **facts**, **opinions**, and **reasoned judgments** in a text

Q: What are an **argument**, **claims**, **reasons**, and **evidence**?

A: The following is an argument for requiring daily PE classes.

> **Claim/Position:** Daily physical education classes should be required for all 6th-grade students.

> **Reason 1:** Requiring daily exercise will help with the obesity problem in our country.

> **Evidence:** In the last 30 years, the number of obese adolescents aged 12 to 19 years has increased from 5.0% to 18.1%.

> **Reason 2:** Physical exercise will result in smarter children and better test scores.

> **Evidence:** Studies from the University of Illinois found that 20 minutes of walking before a test raised children's scores, even if the child was unfit or overweight.

Watch out for the following emotional arguments. They are not as convincing as reasons and evidence.

> **Bandwagon:** All the other schools are requiring daily PE, so we should too. (Appeals to your sense of wanting to be included.)

> **Loaded Words:** The students at our school are fat and lazy. (Uses emotionally-charged words.)

> **Testimonial:** Dr. Sophia Ahmed supports requiring PE every day. (Uses an expert opinion.)

Q: How can I distinguish between **facts**, **opinions**, and a reasoned **judgment**?

A: **Facts** can be proven to be true. An **opinion** is a statement of personal preference. A **reasoned judgment** is a conclusion based upon facts, but it can still be debated.

Dear Superintendent Wright,

1   It's no secret that sixth graders in our school have been unhappy ever since the administration threw recess out of the school day. I'm writing to urge you to change your decision about recess. I understand that schools must teach students more and more every year. Teachers feel they need every minute of the day to fit everything in. However, I think taking recess away has made it harder, not easier, for us to learn.

2   I recently surveyed every sixth grader in our school about recess. Ninety-five percent said that recess was their favorite time of the school day. At recess we were able to spend time with our friends. We are still kids, after all, and kids need to spend time with friends and play. Recess allows us to do something we really enjoy for at least a few minutes every day. With the tons of homework sixth graders have, there is less time for socializing with friends after school. Please allow us to have just a few moments of our favorite activity each day.

3   You must be aware of the research showing that physical exercise helps prepare our minds for learning. We have learned in science that exercise helps blood flow to all parts of our bodies and stimulates cell growth, even *in our brains*. Exercise, then, can help us improve our minds. I admit that when we had recess, not every student used it for exercise. But those of us who did were surely better off for it. P.E. classes are great for jump-starting our brains, but we need to do this every day, not just twice a week.

4   Finally, I'd like to emphasize that all people, kids and adults, need recesses of some kind during their busy days. Here are a couple of examples of how adults have recesses too. During court trials, judges give everyone a recess when they need a break. Many corporations now give employees time during their workday to exercise. This makes the employees happier and more productive. If adults need recesses, then surely kids do as well.

5   Please, let's join the many other school districts that allow their sixth graders to have recess. We need this important break in our stressful days.

Sincerely,
Kristen Johnson

1   What is the student's main purpose for writing the letter?

A to describe sixth graders' unhappiness

B to inform others that there will no longer be recess

C to ask the superintendent some questions

D to convince the superintendent to allow recess again

2 All of the following reasons why sixth graders need recess are given in the passage EXCEPT—

   A It is the favorite part of most sixth graders' day.

   B Everyone—even adults—needs recess of some kind during the day.

   C Recess is one way to keep kids from becoming overweight.

   D Exercise prepares the mind for learning.

3 Which piece of information from the letter supports the author's argument that recess can improve a student's ability to think?

   A Exercise helps stimulate cell growth in the brain.

   B Most kids say recess was their favorite time of day.

   C Some kids choose not to exercise during recess.

   D Kids need to socialize and play.

4 Reread this sentence from the letter.

> It's no secret that sixth graders in our school have been unhappy ever since the administration threw recess out of the school day.

What is the intended effect of saying that administrators *threw recess out*?

   A to inform others of what happened to recess

   B to suggest that administrators acted quickly

   C to suggest a negative feeling

   D to accurately describe how recess was removed

5 Which of the following is a FACT?

   A Ninety-five percent of sixth graders said that recess was their favorite time of day.

   B Kids ought to spend time with friends and play.

   C All people, kids and adults, must have recesses of some kind during their busy days.

   D We need to have recess every day, not just twice a week.

6 Choose paragraph 1, 2, or 3. Evaluate whether the reason presented in the paragraph is convincing or not convincing. Explain whether you think the reason is supported with good evidence, examples, or facts. (5 points)

_____

_____

_____

_____

_____

_____

In **Example 1,** you must determine the author's specific purpose. The author gives a lot of information about recess and its benefits. All the information and descriptions are meant to support the author's argument that recess is important. Her purpose is *to convince the superintendent to allow recess again.* **Choice D** is correct.

Example 2 asks you to identify the reasons used to persuade the principal. It may be helpful to go back and underline the reason in each paragraph. This will help you eliminate the choices one at a time. The only reason not given is **choice C**, *Recess is one way to keep kids from becoming overweight.*

For **Example 3**, you must think about how the author develops a specific **argument**. The **claim** that recess can improve a student's ability to think is developed in paragraph 3 of the letter. In this paragraph, we find the fact that *exercise helps stimulate cell growth in the brain*, or **choice A**.

Example 4 asks you to identify why the writer used the phrase "threw recess out." They are loaded words designed to appeal to negative feelings, or **choice C**.

For **Example 5**, you must distinguish between a **fact** and an **opinion**. Facts can be proven; opinions can't be proven. Opinions often use value words such as *good, bad,* and *beautiful,* or verbs such as *should, must, and ought.* The only answer that can be proven is **choice A**, *Ninety-five percent of sixth-graders said that recess was their favorite time of day.*

To answer **Example 6**, you should choose one of the paragraphs and evaluate whether you think it presents a good reason and explain how the reason is supported. A good answer should explain which paragraph you are evaluating, summarize the reason, explain how the reason is supported, and then explain why you think this is a good or poor reason.

Good: *In paragraph 2, the writer says that kids need recess because most sixth graders enjoy it. The author supports this reason by presenting the results of a survey she took. I do not think this is a convincing argument because it is based on what sixth graders like. Sixth graders would also enjoy drinking pop and eating candy for lunch every day, but the fact is that junk food is unhealthy.*

Poor: *In paragraph 2, the writer says that kids need recess because most sixth graders enjoy it. I guess this is a good reason. I'm in sixth grade, and I'd want to have recess. It doesn't matter if some kids don't like it. I like it.*

◎ Try It On Your Own

Read the following passage and answer the questions that follow.

For years you've felt guilty for eating that chocolate candy bar. Now chocoholics can rejoice! The most delicious candy in the world actually has positive health benefits.

Research shows that chocolate can physically make a person feel better. And you just thought it was all in your head! Well, actually it is. Chocolate is thought to cause certain glands in your body to secrete hormones that make you feel happy. So when you're feeling stressed out or down in the dumps, chocolate can actually pick you up by releasing "feel-good" chemicals into your body.

Chocolate can also be good for your physical health. Doctors at the University of Cologne in Germany recently announced that dark chocolate lowers high blood pressure. Dark chocolate also contains antioxidants that protect the body from heart disease and other ailments.

So go ahead and join the thousands of people eating a candy bar today. It really is good for your body and soul.

7 In the first paragraph, the writer makes the claim that—

    A you should feel guilty for eating chocolate.

    B chocolate is a great snack.

    C chocolate is good for your health.

    D Doctors are encouraging their patients to eat chocolate.

8 What two reasons does the writer give to support his claim? (2 points)

_____

_____

_____

9 The two reasons for eating chocolate are supported mainly with—

    A examples.   **C** opinions.

    B facts.   **D** stories.

10 Which of the following passages appeals to the reader's feelings of not wanting to be left out?

    A *chocolate can actually pick you up by releasing "feel-good" chemicals into your body*

    B *dark chocolate lowers high blood pressure*

    C *The most delicious candy in the world actually has positive health benefits.*

    D *So go ahead and join the thousands of people eating a candy bar today.*

Test-Taking Tips

1 Read carefully and watch for propaganda and persuasion techniques. These techniques are often appealing because they present false or exaggerated statements as facts. Think about whether an author can support statements he or she makes.

2 As you read, think about what the author is saying and why he or she is saying it. An author's purpose will affect the text. Of what is the author trying to persuade you? When you're finished reading, try to decide whether the author was effective in fulfilling his or her purpose.

Go for it!

Unit Six Practice Test

Estimated time: 18 minutes

Directions: Read the passage and study the Web site. Then answer the questions that follow.

April 2012

THE MAYPORT EXAMINER

Racing Dragons

An army of boats races across the harbor to the sound of beating drums. The sea churns as boats tip over and teams row wildly for the finish line. Onlookers eat dumplings as they cheer on friends and family. It's all part of the Tuen Ng, or Dragon Boat Festival. Celebrations like this take place every year all over China. This year, though, the Dragon Boat Festival is coming to Mayport.

The Dragon Boat Festival has been celebrated in China for more than 2000 years. During the festival, the Chinese remember the popular national hero and poet Qu Yuan. According to legend, Qu Yuan was a loyal and honest statesman who advised the emperor wisely. Qu Yuan enjoyed the ruler's trust and respect. He had many jealous rivals, however, who plotted against him. Eventually, the lies of his enemies caused Qu Yuan to fall out of favor with the emperor. He was forced to leave the city. While he was away, he wrote a famous poem called "Li Sao." Finally, to protest the dishonest government, Qu Yuan threw himself into the Mi Lo River. The local townspeople, knowing he was an honorable man, jumped into their boats to save him. The rescuers tried beating drums and striking the water with their oars to keep the fish away from Qu Yuan. After a frantic search, they were unable to find him.

In China, people remember Qu Yuan's life and death during annual Dragon Boat Festivals. Drummers beat loud and pulsing rhythms in time with the oars hitting the water. Families make dumplings, a traditional food eaten every year during the event.

Similar in shape to canoes, the "dragon boats" for the Mayport event are more than 30 feet long. Each is decorated with a carved and painted dragon head attached to the bow. A tail juts from the stern. These decorations are fastened to the boat in a complex ceremony. Once inside the boats, paddlers sit two abreast. Each boat holds twenty paddlers, a drummer, and a person to steer. Teams practice hard for the event, trying to perfect the balance of the boat and the rhythm of the oar strokes. In Hong Kong, the capital of dragon boat racing, more than 100 teams compete. Racers come from as far away as Singapore, England, and the United States. The display of gorgeous boats, intense rowers, and cheering fans makes the Dragon Boat Festival one of China's most unique celebrations.

The growing popularity of dragon boat racing has spread the competition beyond China's borders. Every year, cities around the world hold their own races and festivals. In an effort to introduce the story of Qu Yuan to Mayport, the city is holding its own Dragon Boat Festival on Sunday, June 9. In order to participate in the races, you must assemble a 22-person team. To register your team, please go to <www.mayportdragonraces.com> and click on "Register to Race." Or call 555-100-0101 to request a registration form. Registrations must be completed by May 30, 2012. Local open division winners will go on to represent Mayport in the regional championships later this year.

2011 Youth Race Results			
Lane	**Team**	**Place**	**Time**
1	Park Middle School	2	04:03.22
2	Lincoln Dragons	3	04:03.48
3	Go for the Gold	5	04:20.12
4	Blue Dragons	1	04:02.58
5	Kent Middle School	6	04:47.23
6	Oak Park Rowers	4	04:05.02

All six 2011 youth teams are registered to race again this year.

Back	Forward	Stop	Refresh	Home	Mail

Address: http://www.mayportdragonraces.com   Go ➡

2012 Dragon Boat Festival

Mayport's Chinese Dragon Boat Festival is shaping up to be the most exciting river event of the year! Already, more than twice as many teams have registered for the race. Everyone who likes water sports is planning on racing or cheering for a favorite team. As Mayor Tom Dunn says, "Last year's races were definitely the highlight of the summer." So don't miss out!

The races will be held on Sunday, June 9. Racers must be at the Mayport dock by 8:00 that morning. The first qualifying heat will begin at 9:00. The awards ceremony will be at 1:00, followed by a community picnic. The picnic costs $10 for adults and $5 for children ages 5–12. Children under 5 eat for free.

Each dragon boat comes to life when its eyes are painted in a special ceremony before the race.

Click here to learn more
The Legend Behind the Boats
Festival Food and Fun
Building a Dragon Boat
Calendar
Register to Race
2011 Race Results Adult Division Youth Division

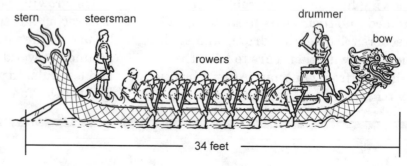

stern   steersman   drummer   bow

rowers

34 feet

1 What is MOST likely the purpose of the newspaper article?

   A to entertain readers with a story about a race

   B to describe a typical dragon boat

   C to inform readers about dragon boats and the dragon boat race

   D to persuade readers to enter the dragon boat race

2 Which information is included in the newspaper article AND on the Web site?

   A diagram of a dragon boat

   B registration form

   C this year's youth race results

   D last year's youth race results

3 Which of the following would be a credible source(s) to find out about the history of the Dragon Boat Festival?

   A the newspaper article

   B the Web site

   C both the newspaper article and the Web site

   D neither

4 Paraphrase the following lines from the newspaper article. (3 points)

   In China, people remember Qu Yuan's life and death during annual Dragon Boat Festivals. Drummers beat loud and pulsing rhythms in time with the oars hitting the water. Families make dumplings, a traditional food eaten every year during the event.

   _____

   _____

   _____

   _____

GO ON

Directions: Read the following letter to the editor and answer the questions that follow.

Dear Mayport Examiner Editor,

1   I would like to encourage everyone to attend the Dragon Boat Festival in Mayport this year.

2   The festival supports our town by bringing thousands of tourists to our community. These tourists eat in our local restaurants and buy merchandise from our local stores. This stimulates our local economy, which has been in a decline for several years.

3   The festival also builds friendships in our community by helping people understand the culture of China. We have a diverse community here in Mayport. People from all over the world have settled in our town, including a sizable population from China. At least for one day, the diverse cultures of our community can come together and celebrate in unity.

4   Finally, the festival is not only fun, but also educational. Every year my children learn about the history of China by attending this event. They eat delicious dumplings, hear Chinese drummers, and experience amazing artwork. Often teachers at school have the children write about what they experienced at the festival. Doing away with the festival would hurt the future of our country—our children.

5   I hope everyone attends the Dragon Boat Festival this year. It really is the best family and community event in Mayport.

Tasha Adams

5 Which of the following reasons to attend the Dragon Boat festival is NOT used by the letter writer?

  A The festival is educational for children.

  B The festival gives Chinese artists a place to perform.

  C The festival unites the city of Mayport.

  D The festival brings money from tourism into the town.

6 Which of the following facts would support the reason developed in paragraph 2?

  A The festival cost the city $375,000 to put on last year.

  B Ten thousand people of Chinese heritage live in the city of Mayport.

  C The festival brought in $500,000 in tourist revenue last year.

  D Mayport is the only city in the state with a Dragon Boat Festival.

7 Reread the following sentence.

Doing away with the festival would hurt the future of our country—our children.

This is an example of—

A a fact.

B bandwagon technique.

C an emotional appeal.

D a testimonial by a famous person.

8 In paragraphs 2, 3, and 4 the letter writer develops claims to support her argument. Choose one of the paragraphs and evaluate the writer's claim. Be sure to explain if she uses facts, opinions, emotional appeals, or other evidence to support the main idea of the paragraph. (3 points)

_____

_____

_____

_____

_____

_____

_____

_____

_____

_____

_____

_____

_____

STOP

Points Earned/Total = _____/12

Language
Lesson

13

Pronoun Case

Review the Standards (L.6.1.a–b, W.6.5)
- Use **pronouns** in the proper **case**
- Use **intensive pronouns**

Q: How do I make sure **pronouns** are in the correct **case**?

A: A **pronoun** is a word used in place of a noun. It is important to use the proper pronoun **case** when writing and speaking. Study the following chart:

Case	Explanation	Example Pronouns	Example Sentences
Subjective	shows who or what does something	*I, we, you, he, she, they*	**She** and **I** volunteered to work at the shelter.
Objective	shows to whom or to what something is being done	*me, us, you, them, him*	Antonio read the announcement to **her** and **me**.
Possessive	shows possession of something	*mine, our, your, her, his, their*	Rudy left **his** football in **our** yard.

Q: How do I use **intensive pronouns** correctly?

A: Intensive pronouns are formed by adding *-self* or *-selves* to certain personal pronouns: *myself, yourself, himself, herself,* and *themselves.* Use an intensive pronoun immediately after the noun to which it refers. Never use them as a subject.

Examples:

Maya **herself** made the cake for the wedding.

The players **themselves** picked up all the trash on the football field.

Hint

Never use *hisself* or *theirselves.*

Try It

The paragraph below has three pronoun mistakes. Draw a line through each mistake and write the correction above it.

Please give Donnetta and I a chance to try out for the basketball team. Last year her and I shot baskets every day. Myself ran three miles a day to keep in shape. Donnetta thinks that we perform better than some of the current team members.

The first pronoun mistake is the use of *Donnetta and I* in the first sentence. This sentence needs an object for the verb *give*. It is helpful to read the sentence without the phrase *Donnetta and;* for example, *Please give I a chance to try out for the team.* You can hear that *Please give I* is incorrect. Cross out the *I* and write *me* above it.

The next mistake is *her and I. Her* and *I* are the subjects of the sentence. However, *her* is not a subjective case pronoun. Cross *her* out and write *she.*

The final mistake is in the sentence *Myself ran three miles a day to keep in shape. Myself* is an intensive pronoun used to emphasize who is doing the action. It should not be used as a subject. It should be corrected by rewriting the sentence as *I myself ran three miles a day to keep in shape.*

◎ Try It On Your Own

The paragraph below has three pronoun mistakes. Draw a line through each mistake and write the correction above it.

Joel and me go hiking almost every weekend. Sometimes our friends Ginny and Ross go with ourselves. They theirselves have climbed three mountains over 14,000 feet high. We enjoy finding examples of leaves and wildflowers. You are welcome to come hiking with us sometime.

Pronoun Shifts

Review the Standards (L.6.1.c–d, W.6.5)

- Recognize and correct inappropriate pronoun shifts and **vague** pronouns

Q: How do I correct shifts in pronouns?

A: A **pronoun** must agree with the word it is replacing, or its antecedent.

Incorrect: James and DeShawn can't find **his** bikes.

Correct: James and DeShawn can't find **their** bikes.

Incorrect: If a person wants to succeed in school, **you** must study hard.

Correct: If a person wants to succeed in school, **he or she** must study hard.

If you want to succeed in school, **you** must study hard.

Q: How do I correct **vague pronouns**?

A: **Vague pronouns** are confusing because they don't refer to a specific noun.

Examples:

I don't think **they** should put violent shows on TV. (Who are *they*? The networks? The television executives?)

I put my iPod in the car, but now **it** is gone. (Does *it* refer to the iPod or the car?)

Correct these sentences by changing the vague pronoun to a specific noun.

I don't think **the networks** should put violent shows on TV.

I put my iPod in the car, but now my **iPod** is gone.

Try It

Read each sentence. Choose the word or words that best complete each sentence.

1 Polar bears, unlike ____ cousins the brown bears, do not usually hibernate in the winter.

    A his

    B its

    C their

    D our

2 The janitor searched for my lost scarf, but he could not find ____.

    A ours

    B him

    C them

    D it

3 If you want to travel to Mexico this summer, ____ will have to get a passport.

    A you

    B a person

    C they

    D we

When answering questions about pronouns, you should always find the pronoun's antecedent. Then you must find the answer choice that agrees with the antecedent in gender, number, and person. For **Example 1**, the antecedent is polar bears, which is plural. You can eliminate choices A and B because they are singular pronouns. *Our* is in first person and doesn't fit the point of view of the sentence. The correct answer is **choice C**.

In **Example 2**, the missing pronoun is referring to a scarf. The correct pronoun is *it*, **choice D**.

Example 3 is written in second person (*you*). In order to avoid shifting tenses, the correct answer is **choice A**, *you*.

Read each sentence. Choose the word or words that best complete each sentence.

4　Mom and Dad packed ____ bags for vacation.

   A　his

   B　her

   C　their

   D　them

5　Crack the eggshells, separate the yolks from the whites, and place ____ in the cake batter.

   A　it

   B　them

   C　the whites

   D　the eggshells

6　If someone came to the party now, ____ wouldn't find any food left to eat.

   A　he or she

   B　you

   C　him or her

   D　their

Test-Taking Tips

1　When editing a passage for pronoun usage, read the passage silently to yourself. Underline any pronouns that don't sound right.

2　If a sentence has a noun and a pronoun joined by *and*, such as *Jake and her repaired the damaged tire*, try reading the sentence without *Jake and*. You wouldn't say *Her repaired the damaged tire*. You know that the sentence should be *Jake and she repaired the damaged tire*.

3　Always look for the antecedent to which the pronoun refers. Remember that pronouns must agree with their antecedents in gender, number, and person. Watch for inappropriate shifts within a sentence.

Go for it!

Unit Seven Practice Test

Estimated time: 10 minutes

Directions: Read the following passage. If the underlined words are correct, write C on the numbered line. If they are incorrect, write the correction on the line.

Dear Emily,

   Mom and Dad told (1) John and I that you are planning your birthday party this year. You will need both money and advice so (2) me wanted to give you (3) it.

   Planning a party can be a big chore, but it can also be a lot of fun. The first thing you should do is plan the theme of the party. (4) A person can get ideas by walking up and down the aisles of (5) their local party store. Next think about invitations. Using the Internet, (6) you herself can send out e-vites. This will allow you to save money for food and decorations. You can also save money by asking your guests to bring (7) his or her favorite snack food to the party.

   (8) John and I will plan on coming to the party early so we can help decorate the house.

Love,

Bethany

1 _____

2 _____

3 _____

4 _____

5 _____

6 _____

7 _____

8 _____

Points Earned/Total = _____/8

Language
Lesson

15

Capitalization, Punctuation, and Spelling

Review the Standards (L.6.1.e, L.6.2.a–b)

- Use **commas**, **parentheses**, and **dashes** to set off **nonrestrictive/parenthetical** elements
- Use correct **capitalization** and **spelling**
- Identify and use standard English

Q: What are **nonrestrictive** and **parenthetical** elements?

A: Nonrestrictive means that the phrase or clause does not change the meaning of the sentence. It is not essential to the meaning of the sentence. See the examples below.

Nonrestrictive: My sister, who is a very good speller, didn't turn in her registration for the spelling bee on time.

Restrictive: The student who spells the most words correctly will go on to the state spelling bee.

Parenthetical expressions are inserted into the sentence but are not directly related to the subject at hand.

Q: When do I use commas, parentheses, and dashes with nonrestrictive and parenthetical elements?

A: In most cases, commas are used with nonrestrictive clauses. Other parenthetical information may be set off with parentheses or dashes. Study the chart below and on the next page.

Punctuation Mark	Explanation	Example
Commas (,)	• use to enclose information that is loosely related to the rest of the sentence, yet is nonessential • commas are most often used to set off nonrestrictive clauses	Ms. Jackson, **who is my favorite teacher**, teaches math and science classes.

Punctuation Mark	Explanation	Example
Parentheses ( )	• use to enclose information that is not essential to the meaning of the sentence but that adds an interesting point • often used with examples, directions, and explanations • also used for dates	The poems of Edgar Allan Poe **("The Raven," "The Bells")** often contain sound imagery that heightens the emotional feel of the poetry.
Dashes (—)	• use to signal a break in the train of thought	I think the test is on Thursday—**no Friday**—of this week.

Q: What are the rules for correct **capitalization** and **punctuation**?

A: These charts will help you review **capitalization** and **punctuation** rules.

Basics of Capitalization

☞ Capitalize the first word in a sentence, in a quotation, and in the salutation and closing of a letter.

> The instructor said, "Arrange the chairs in a semicircle."
>
> My dear Mrs. Foley,
>
> With love,

☞ Capitalize the first word, the last word, and every important word in the title of a song, story, play, book, or movie.

> A New Settlement on the Frontier

☞ Capitalize the names of days, months, holidays, streets, natural features, titles, and specific regions.

> Fourth of July
>
> Rocky Mountains
>
> Thanksgiving is always on Thursday.
>
> The James River has flooded.
>
> Dr. Johnson
>
> the Midwest

☞ Capitalize proper adjectives, which refer to people and nationalities, and the names of political and religious groups.

> Canadian climate
>
> an Arabian horse
>
> Methodists and Baptists

GO ON

Try It

Directions: Read each question and choose the best answer.

1   Complete the sentence below by choosing the word that
    is spelled correctly.

    The football _____ was filled with fans.

    A stadeum   **C** stadium
    B staddeum   **D** staedium

2   Which sentence is punctuated correctly?

    A Marks three dogs raced around the yard.
    B Marks' three dogs raced around the yard.
    C Marks three dogs' raced around the yard.
    D Mark's three dogs raced around the yard.

3   Which of the following sentences is NOT punctuated correctly?

    A Edgar Allan Poe—1809–1849—was famous for mysterious stories and his
           strange behavior.
    B In 1846, Edgar Allan Poe moved to a cottage at Fordham (now part of
           New York City).
    C Poe married his cousin Virginia Clemm, who was only 13 at the time
           of their marriage.
    D Poe is still considered to be one of the best—if not the greatest—
           short story writers.

4   Study the sentence below. Then answer the question that follows.

    My favorite book is The Wind in the Willows.

    In this sentence, the word *Wind* is capitalized because it—

    A is a proper noun.
    B is an important word in a title.
    C is a proper adjective.
    D begins the sentence.

    Some questions will test your ability to spell. **Example 1** asks you to identify the word
that is spelled correctly. *Stadium* is the correct spelling, or **choice C**.
    To answer **Example 2**, you must understand how to show ownership. Mark is the
only one who owns something in this sentence—the dogs. To show that the dogs belong to
Mark, you must add an apostrophe (') plus *s*. Choice A is wrong because the apostrophe is
missing. Choice B is wrong because the apostrophe should be before the *s*, not after it. The
apostrophe only goes after the *s* when the word that names who or what owns something
is plural and ends with *s*. (*The two boys' dogs raced around the yard*.) Choice C is incorrect
because nothing belongs to the dogs, so an apostrophe is not needed. **Choice D is correct**.

© **Perfection Learning® No reproduction permitted.**

To answer **Example 3**, you must think about how commas, dashes, and parentheses are used. All of them can be used to set off nonrestrictive or parenthetical elements. As you read choice A, you realize that parentheses, not dashes, are used to set off dates. The punctuation in the other choices is correct. The correct answer is **choice A**.

Example 4 tests both your understanding of capitalization and your ability to write a title. In the title of a book, article, story, song, or movie, the first word, last word, and all the important words in between are capitalized. The only words that are not capitalized are words such as *the, and, in, for,* and *by*—unless they are the first or last word of the title. **Choice B** is correct.

◎ Try It On Your Own

5 Choose the underlined word that is NOT spelled correctly in the sentence.

Luke's <u>goals</u> for the year were to join <u>orchestra</u>, <u>participate</u> in a school sport, and <u>earn</u> better grades.

A goals
B orchestra
C participate
D earn

6 Which sentence is punctuated correctly?

A Grandpa gave me a huge present but he said I had to wait until my birthday to open it.
B Grandpa gave me a huge present, but he said I had to wait until my birthday to open it.
C Grandpa gave me a huge present; but he said I had to wait until my birthday to open it.
D Grandpa gave me a huge present: but he said I had to wait until my birthday to open it.

7 Which sentence uses capitalization correctly?

A The conference was held in Chicago, illinois.
B Dave met his Uncle at a restaurant on State Street.
C They decided to visit the Sears Tower.
D There were american flags in front of the building.

8 Which sentence is punctuated correctly?

A "The meeting is canceled said Franco.
B "The meeting is canceled, said Franco.
C "The meeting is canceled, said Franco."
D "The meeting is canceled," said Franco.

Hint

For school and other formal writing situations, you should use **standard English** and **conventional language** and avoid slang and informal language such as *cool, ain't,* and *y'all.*

Sentence Patterns

Review the Standards (L.6.3.a, W.6.5)
• Vary **sentence patterns**
• Edit writing

Q: How do I vary **sentence patterns**?

A: The following paragraph is boring because the sentences are all alike. The paragraph is redundant because information is repeated.

Sally did the laundry. Joe did the laundry. Joe vacuumed the carpet. Sally washed the dishes. All the chores were done. All the chores were done before their mom returned home.

Varying the types and lengths of sentences creates interesting writing. Sometimes you may need to combine shorter sentences by combining subjects, predicates, or modifiers.

Sally and Joe did the laundry. While Sally washed the dishes, Joe vacuumed the carpet. All the chores were done before their mom returned home.

 Try It

Directions: Read each group of sentences below. Rewrite the sentences as one sentence. Try to vary the sentence structure as much as possible.

1 Joe likes soccer. Steven likes soccer.

_____

_____

2 Rita likes to swim. Sally likes to fish. Both Rita and Sally like to go to the lake.

_____

_____

Directions: Read the following paragraph, and then answer the question that follows.

¹At first the Internet was used only by scientists. ²Now many other people use it. ³It makes all kinds of information available to people all over the world.

3 Which of the following best combines sentences 1 and 2 into one sentence?

  A At first the Internet was used only by scientists, but now many other people use it too.

  B Scientists and the Internet are used by many other people now.

  C Now the Internet is used by many other people, but not by scientists.

  D At first scientists and many other people used the Internet.

Both sentences in **Example 1** have the same pattern. You could combine them by using a compound subject: *Joe and Steven like soccer*.

The sentences in **Example 2** are very redundant. Think about how you can make the sentences more interesting. Try changing the third sentence into a prepositional phrase and using it at the beginning of a new compound sentence: *At the lake, Rita likes to swim, but Sally likes to fish*.

Read the answer choices for **Example 3**. Choices B, C, and D incorrectly state the information in the paragraph. **Choice A** correctly shows the relationship between the scientists who first used the Internet and the people who use the Internet now.

◎ Try It On Your Own

¹Radio was invented in the first half of the 20th century. ²Television was invented in the first half of the 20th century. ³These devices made mass communication possible. ⁴The Internet was a later invention. ⁵It has improved communication even more.

4 Which of the following best combines sentences 1 and 2?

  A The first half of the 20th century invented radio and television.

  B Radio and television were invented in the first half of the 20th century.

  C Radio invented television in the first half of the 20th century.

  D Radio was the first half of the 20th century, and so was television.

5 Which of the following best combines sentences 4 and 5?

  A The Internet has improved communication as a later invention.

  B The Internet was invented later, it has improved communication even more.

  C The Internet, a later invention, has improved communication even more.

  D Communication on the Internet improved even more later.

GO ON

6 Rewrite the following paragraph by combining sentences to make the writing clearer and more interesting. (3 points)

The cartoonist did drawings of all the guests. The drawings were clever. He focused on features like heavy eyebrows and long necks. He exaggerated them in his drawings. These drawings are called *caricatures*. All the guests liked the caricatures.

_____

_____

_____

_____

_____

_____

_____

Test-Taking Tips

1 Check each word in a sentence carefully, looking for errors in capitalization and spelling. Remember, capitalization can occur even in the middle of a sentence, so every word must be checked.

2 When rewriting or combining sentences, look for repeated ideas that you can combine as compound subjects or verbs. Contrasting ideas can be rewritten as a compound sentence joined by *but*.

Go for it!

Unit Eight Practice Test

Estimated time: 10 minutes

Directions: Read each question and choose the best answer.

1 Which sentence is punctuated correctly?

  A The optometrist asked, Can you read the chart?

  B The optometrist asked, "Can you read the chart?"

  C "The optometrist asked, Can you read the chart?"

  D "The optometrist" asked "Can you read the chart?

2 Complete the sentence below by choosing the word that is spelled correctly.

She peered over the side of a _____-foot drop.

  A forty

  B fortey

  C fourty

  D fordy

3 Which sentence uses capitalization correctly?

  A Last Memorial day we visited the cemetery.

  B We put flowers on grandpa Munoz's grave.

  C He fought in the Korean War.

  D Mama said, "He was a wonderful Man."

4 Which sentence is punctuated correctly?

  A One day after school; Sarah and I decided to bake cookies.

  B We found a recipe in *Home Cooking* one of my favorite cookbooks.

  C The recipe called for the following: eggs, flour, sugar, and vanilla.

  D I will send some cookies to my grandmother in New York, City.

5 Which sentence is punctuated correctly?

  A Darla's book—*The Hunger Games*—was overdue at the library.

  B The book, which Darla didn't have time to read, was due last week.

  C After Darla got to the library—she discovered that her money a dollar in quarters was gone.

  D The librarian (on duty that day) said that Darla could pay the fine later.

GO ON

6 Rewrite the following paragraph by combining sentences to make the writing clearer and more interesting. (3 points)

> Our class took a field trip to the art museum. The special exhibit at the museum was about Vincent van Gogh and Paul Gauguin. We learned about these artists. They worked together for a time. We saw how each one's ideas influenced the other. We also saw how each one's painting styles influenced the other. We could compare the paintings that each artist did of the same scene. We learned a lot.

_____

_____

_____

_____

_____

_____

_____

STOP

Points Earned/Total = _____/8

Language
Lesson

17

Word Analysis

Review the Standards (L.6.4.b, L.6.5.b)

- Use affixes and **roots** as clues to the meaning of a word
- Use the relationship between words to understand their meanings

---

Q: How can understanding **prefixes**, **suffixes**, and **roots** help me determine the meaning of words?

A: Knowing the meanings of common **prefixes**, **suffixes**, and **roots** will help you determine the meanings of unknown words. The word *submerge,* for example, is formed by combining the Latin prefix *sub* (under) and the Latin root *merge* (dive). Study the chart below.

bi (two)	+	*ped* (feet)	=	biped
astro (star)	+	*nomy* (science of)	=	astronomy
phono (sound)	+	*graph* (write)	=	phonograph
con (against)	+	*dict* (speak)	=	contradict
geo (earth)	+	*logy* (science of)	=	geology
auto (self)	+	*mob* (move)	=	automobile
ex (from)	+	*port* (carry)	=	export
re (again)	+	*mem* (keep in mind)	=	remember
thermo (heat)	+	*meter* (measure)	=	thermometer

Q: How can I determine the relationship between pairs of words?

A: Look at the following word pairs, or word analogies.

WARM : HOT :: cool : cold

The above example reads "Warm is to hot as cool is to cold." In other words, the word *warm* has the same relationship to the word *hot* as the word *cool* has to the word *cold*. To answer analogy questions, you should try to figure out the relationship between the first two words. Then read your answer choices and find the one that most closely fits the relationship of the first two words. In this example, we understand that *hot* is a synonym for *warm*, and *cool* is a synonym for *cold*.

GO ON

Common Types of Analogies	
Analogy	**Example**
cause : effect	cold : frostbite
word : synonym	mistake : error
word : antonym	strong : weak
part : whole	nose : face
item : category	carrot : vegetable

 Try It

Directions: Read the following passage, and then answer the questions.

Marine **biologists** are amazed by the ability of the common octopus to fend off its predators. These intelligent **invertebrates** have specialized pigment cells in their skin that allow them to match the colors, patterns, and even textures of their surroundings. If a shark or eel does happen to discover an octopus, the octopus will expel a cloud of black ink to confuse and disorient the attacker. If an **attacker** is able to penetrate these defenses, an octopus has the ability to lose one of its eight arms and then regrow it later.

1 Based on what you know about the *octopus*, the Greek prefix *octo-* means—

   A sea.   **C** eight.
   B animal.   **D** large.

2 Which of the following BEST describes the origin of the word *biologist*?

   A The word comes from the Greek prefix *bi-*, meaning "two," and the Greek root *-logy*, meaning "science of."
   B The word comes from the Greek prefix *bi-*, meaning "two," and the Greek root *-log*, meaning "word."
   C The word comes from the Greek prefix *bio-*, meaning "life," and the Greek root *-logy*, meaning "science of."
   D The word comes from the Greek prefix *bio-*, meaning "life," and the Greek root *-log*, meaning "word."

Directions: Complete the following analogies.

3 INTELLIGENT : SMART :: confuse :

   A attack
   B disorient
   C help
   D ink

4 LEG : HUMAN :: arm :

   A invertebrate
   B shark
   C octopus
   D skin

Example 1 asks you to think about what you already know to determine the meaning of the Greek prefix *octo-*. To answer the question, first read all four choices. Then ask yourself what you know about the octopus. It is a large sea animal that has eight long arms, or tentacles, so all four choices tell something about the octopus. However, only one characteristic makes it different from other large sea animals—its eight legs. **Choice C**, *eight*, is correct. Other words that share this prefix include *octagon* and *octave*.

To answer **Example 2**, you must think about what the word *biologist* means, and then choose the word parts that most closely apply to that meaning. Biology is the study of living things, and a biologist is a scientist who studies living things. **Choice C** is correct.

Example 3 asks you to complete an analogy. Think about the relationship between the words *intelligent* and *smart*. They are similar in meaning, so you need to find a synonym for the word *confuse*. The word with the similar meaning is **choice B**, *disorient*.

In **Example 4**, the relationship given is a part to a whole. The correct answer is **choice C**, *octopus*.

◎ Try It On Your Own

5   Which word from the passage comes from the Latin root *mar*, meaning "sea"?

    A *remarkable* **C** *marine*
    B *arm*   **D** *marvelous*

6   If you know that the word *vertebrate* means "having a spinal column," you can figure out that the word *invertebrate* means—

    A "not having a spinal column."
    B "not living in the water."
    C "having an external spinal column."
    D "causing to have a spinal column."

7   In which of the following words does the suffix *-er* mean the same thing as in the word *attacker*?

    A teacher   **C** letter
    B happier   **D** bigger

Directions: Complete the following analogies.

8   OCTOPUS : INK :: bee :

    A wing
    B hive
    C honey
    D sting

9   LIGHT : DARK :: predator :

    A invertebrate
    B prey
    C shark
    D attacker

Language Lesson

18

Reference Materials and Multiple Meanings

Review the Standards (L.6.4.c–d)

- Consult **reference materials** to find the pronunciation, part of speech, or meaning of a word
- Determine the meaning of multiple-meaning words and phrases

Q: What information can I find in **reference materials** such as **dictionaries, glossaries,** and **thesauruses**?

A: **Dictionaries** give you the most information about a word, including part of speech, pronunciation, and definitions.

Glossaries are a kind of shortened dictionary found in a book, containing only words related to the content of the book.

Thesauruses can help you find synonyms or antonyms of a word.

 Try It

Directions: Use the dictionary and glossary samples to answer the questions below.

> **blun·der** [blun´ der] *n.* A foolish or careless mistake.
> **board** [bôrd] *n.* **1.** A thin, wide piece of wood for use in building. **2.** A tablet or frame on which pieces from a game are moved. **3.** A table on which to serve food. **4.** A group of persons managing a company or organization.

Glossary

double	actor who stands in for another actor
gaffer	the chief lighting technician for a film
pan	the action of the camera rotating on its axis
score	musical piece of a movie's soundtrack

1 The words *blunder* and *board* are both what part of speech?

   A verb

   B noun

   C preposition

   D adjective

2 Which definition of *board* is used in the sentence below?

Take out the backgammon <u>board</u> *so we can play.*

   A definition 1
   B definition 2
   C definition 3
   D definition 4

3 What is a *gaffer*?

   A actor
   B movie director
   C giraffe
   D chief lighting technician

Example 1 asks you to find the part of speech in the dictionary entries for *blunder* and *board*. After each boldface entry word, there is a pronunciation and then a part of speech. An abbreviation is given for the word *noun* (*n.*). Other parts of speech are verb (v.), adjective (adj.), or adverb (adv.). The correct answer is **choice B**.

For **Example 2**, you must look at the context of the sentence and then use the dictionary entry to find the correct meaning of the word *board*. You may not be familiar with the word *backgammon*, but you do know the word *play* often refers to playing a game. You can conclude that the correct definition is 2, or **choice B**.

To answer **Example 3**, you must use the Glossary to find that a *gaffer* is a lighting technician, or **choice D**.

 Try It On Your Own

Directions: Use the following dictionary and glossary entries to answer questions 4–6.

---

blun·der [blun' der] *n.* A foolish or careless mistake.
board [bôrd] *n.* **1.** A thin, wide piece of wood for use in building.
   2. A tablet or frame on which pieces from a game are moved.
   3. A table on which to serve food. **4.** A group of persons managing
   a company or organization.

Glossary

double	actor who stands in for another actor
gaffer	the chief lighting technician for a film
pan	the action of the camera rotating on its axis
score	musical piece of a movie's soundtrack

4 What is a *blunder*?

   A a heavy thunderstorm

   B a kind of rifle

   C an error

   D an ice-making machine

5 Which definition for the word *board* is used in the sentence below?

The school <u>board</u> decided to start school on September 2 next year.

   A definition 1

   B definition 2

   C definition 3

   D definition 4

6 Which word from the Glossary is missing from the following sentence?

The _____ for the new movie was written and performed by the rock band U2.

   A double

   B gaffer

   C pan

   D score

Test-Taking Tips

1 For multiple-meaning words, decide what the underlined word means in the sentence. Then look for the definition that best matches that meaning.

2 Look at what role the word plays in the sentence. Asking yourself if the word functions as a noun, verb, adjective, or adverb in the sentence will help you narrow down the possible meanings.

Go for it!

Unit Nine Practice Test

Estimated time: 15 minutes

Directions: Read the passage. Then answer the questions that follow.

1   During the 1700s, disputes between France, Spain, and Britain began in the colonies and eventually spilled over into Europe. These disputes came to be known as the French and Indian War (1754–1763). When Great Britain won the war in 1763, King George III unwisely decided to tax the American <u>colonists</u> to pay for troops that he had stationed there. This decision, along with a number of other laws passed by British Parliament, increased Great Britain's control over the colonies. Many colonists felt that Great Britain should not be allowed to tax the colonies, or <u>enact</u> other forms of law, without the colonies having some say in the matter. Great Britain felt otherwise, and as a result, tension between the two sides began to <u>mount</u>.

2   In 1774, the colonists formed the first Continental Congress. The <u>delegates</u> of this Congress decided that if Great Britain did not change some of their "intolerable" laws, the colonists would refuse to trade with them. Great Britain would not relent, however, and on April 18, 1775, sent troops to march against Concord. That night, Paul Revere and William Dawes were <u>dispatched</u> to warn the patriots. The next day, fighting broke out in Lexington, and the Revolutionary War began.

3   Six years and many battles later, the colonists accomplished a <u>Herculean task</u>. The small American army defeated a <u>large</u> British force at Yorktown, Virginia.

1 Noting the meaning of the prefix *en-*, what does the word <u>enact</u> mean?

   A to move inside a space

   B to put into action

   C to act again

   D to complete an action

2 What does the suffix *-ist* help you understand about <u>colonists</u>?

   A Colonists are part of a colony.

   B Colonists leave a colony.

   C Colonists live outside of a colony.

   D Colonists do not believe in colonization.

3 Based on what you read, what is a <u>Herculean task</u>?

   A an extremely difficult task

   B a senseless task

   C a task that is done over and over

   D a poorly done task

4 Study the thesaurus entry.

LARGE	
adjective	
bulky	A big, awkward size. *The bulky package didn't fit in the trunk.*
roomy	Having a lot of space. *The car's interior was roomy.*
substantial	Having a great number or area. *A substantial crowd watched the game.*
wide	Having a great measure across. *The path is six feet wide.*

Which word is the BEST replacement for <u>large</u> in paragraph 3?

   A bulky

   B roomy

   C substantial

   D wide

5 Study the dictionary entry.

> **del·e·gate** *n.* (del´ ə git) **1.** A person given the power to represent others. *Our group sent two delegates to the meeting.* *v.* (del´ ə gāt) **2.** To send a person as a representative. *Our group will delegate one member to attend the meeting.* **3.** To give your power to another so that he or she can act for you. *The teacher decided to delegate the job of keeping the class quiet to one student.*

Which definition BEST fits the use of the word <u>delegates</u> in the second paragraph?

A definition 1

B definition 2

C definition 3

D none of the above

6 Reread this sentence from paragraph 1.

Great Britain felt otherwise, and as a result, tension between the two sides began to <u>mount</u>.

What does the word <u>mount</u> mean, as it is used in this sentence?

A increase

B a base or stand used for support

C get on

D a large hill

Directions: Complete the following analogies based upon words from the passage.

---

7 COLONISTS : AMERICA :: British :

A Colonies

B Great Britain

C British Parliament

D King George

8 LEAVE : GO :: dispatch :

A send

B sign

C stop

D tax

Points Earned/Total = _____/8

Mastery Test: Part 1

Estimated time: 30 minutes

Directions: Read the passage. Then answer the questions that follow.

---

1 Alex shivered and snuggled into the blankets. She rolled over and closed her eyes, but she couldn't fall asleep. Something had made a noise somewhere in the house. The sounds were barely <u>audible</u>—a faint noise like fingernails scratching a chalkboard, followed by tiny footsteps. Alex sat up in bed, her heart beating fast. She knew that her parents were fast asleep. If she woke them up, they probably would tell her it was just the wind. So again she tried to fall asleep, but it was no use. Alex was up late wondering about the sounds.

2 The next day at school during lunch, she told her friends what she had heard.

3 "Do you think it was a prowler?" asked Eliza.

4 "I bet it was a ghost!" said Miko. "That's so cool!"

5 "I don't know what it was," Alex said, "but it sure was weird. And I'm going to need your help to figure it out." Her friends nodded their heads in agreement. "Emergency sleepover party at my house tonight," Alex said. "We're going to get to the bottom of this mystery."

6 That night Eliza, Miko, Becky, Sarah, and Olivia came to Alex's house. The girls had a taco dinner together and watched a movie. Afterward, it was time to go up to Alex's room and get ready for bed. When they all were finally lying down, the girls became quiet and listened. They heard nothing for a long, long time. Miko declared that she was bored. Just then, they heard a scratch. *Scratch, scratch, scratch.* The girls listened closely and then made a plan to explore the house in pairs. That way no one would have to be alone.

7 Becky and Eliza carried a flashlight into the cold, dark basement. Sarah and Olivia searched the attic. Miko and Alex started in the living room. They were the first to hear the scratching sounds again. Miko almost screamed, but Alex clamped her hand over Miko's mouth. "Shhhh," she said. Then they heard tiny footsteps.

8 "We're being followed!" said Miko. Alex shushed her again. They heard what sounded like soft voices. Miko's eyes grew wide.

9 "OK, I've had enough of this," said Alex as she flipped on the light. The two girls stopped in their tracks.

10 There on the table were two squirrels, eating leftover corn chips from the girls' dinner. Miko and Alex looked at each other. Then they burst into nervous laughter. "Well," said Alex, "there's our ghost!"

116

1 The point of view of the story is—

   A first person told by Alex.

   B first person told by Miko.

   C third person told by an outside narrator.

   D both first person and third person.

2 Knowing that the Latin root *aud* means "to hear" helps you understand that the word *audible* means—

   A almost silent.

   B able to be heard.

   C in the ears.

   D unable to be heard.

3 The dialogue in paragraphs 2–5 is important to the story because it helps the reader understand that Alex's friends—

   A think that Alex is lying about the sounds.

   B are timid and nervous.

   C want to help their friend solve the mystery.

   D think that Alex should forget about the noises.

4 Which of the following supporting details should NOT be included in a summary of the story?

   A Alex's friends stayed overnight to help her get to the bottom of the mystery.

   B Becky and Eliza explored the basement with a flashlight.

   C The girls heard scratching noises.

   D Alex told her friends about the mysterious noises.

5 How does Alex change from the beginning to the end of the story?

   A She makes more friends.

   B She stops listening to Miko's ideas about ghosts.

   C She overcomes her fear of the noises in her house.

   D She learns to trust her parents' ideas about noises in the night.

6 The main conflict of the story is—

   A Miko doesn't want to stop talking.

   B Alex is afraid to talk to her parents about the noises.

   C the squirrels are trying to get into Alex's house to find food.

   D Alex is afraid of noises she hears in her house at night.

7 This diagram shows the plot of the story.

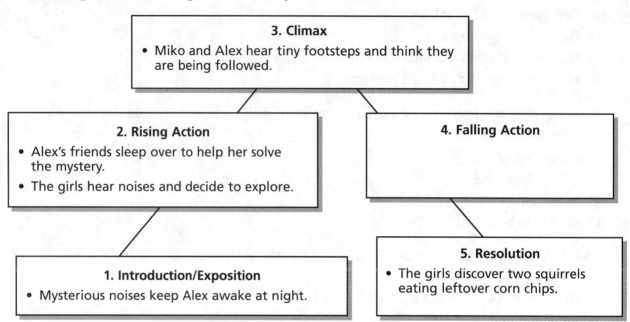

3. Climax
- Miko and Alex hear tiny footsteps and think they are being followed.

2. Rising Action
- Alex's friends sleep over to help her solve the mystery.
- The girls hear noises and decide to explore.

4. Falling Action

1. Introduction/Exposition
- Mysterious noises keep Alex awake at night.

5. Resolution
- The girls discover two squirrels eating leftover corn chips.

Which sentence belongs in the area marked "Falling Action"?

A Becky and Eliza explore the basement.

B Miko says she is bored.

C Sarah and Olivia search the attic.

D Alex turns on the light.

8 A theme of this story is that—

A squirrels are pests.

B sleepovers can be boring.

C things aren't always what they seem to be.

D it is silly to believe in ghosts.

Directions: Read the following poem and answer the questions that follow.

Noises, noises in the night,
Causing me to quake with fright.
I yank the covers over my head
And burrow down into my bed.

5 A *scratch*, a *thump*, a *moan*, a *creak*
Was it the wind that made that *shriek*?
Or a banshee come to haunt my room,
A ghost condemned to unending doom.

The scuttle of claws upon the floor,
10 A tapping at my closet door,
I imagine a monster come to dine;
I can feel his hot breath upon my spine.

Tho' I know what scares me in the night
Will somehow vanish with daylight,
15 For now my blankets are my shield;
I'm safe as long as I'm concealed.

Like a rabbit hidden underground,
Away from all those frightening sounds.
I will never give up the fight
20 Against the noises in the night.

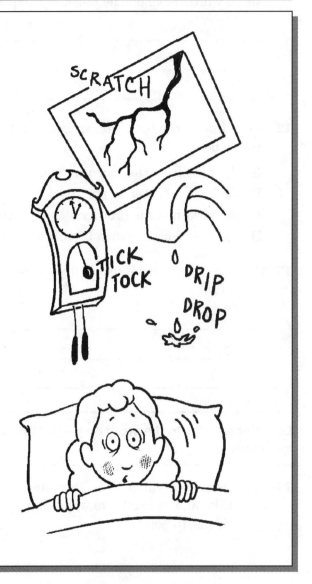

9 Which of the following has the same connotation as the word *yank* in line 3?

A pull

B draw

C drag

D jerk

10 The figurative language in line 15 implies that the speaker—

A thinks the blankets will protect him.

B feels brave like a knight going to battle.

C is cold and needs more blankets.

D plans to fight the monster in his room.

11 Explain why the writer uses the words *scratch, thump, moan*, and *creak*. What impact do these words have on the mood of the poem? (3 points)

_____

_____

_____

12 Based upon the text, we can infer that the hot breath the writer describes might really be—

A the heat from the morning sun.

B air from a heater in the room.

C the breath of his brother sleeping next to him.

D the heat from his own breathing underneath the covers.

13 Analyze the author's use of first-person point of view. What does it add to the poem? (3 points)

_____

_____

_____

Directions: Refer to the story on page 116 and the poem on page 119 to answer the following question.

14 Compare and contrast the story and the poem you just read. Explain at least one way they are alike and at least two ways they are different. Give evidence from the texts to support your ideas. (5 points)

_____

_____

_____

_____

_____

_____

_____

Take a break. Then go on to Part 2.

Directions: Read the passage. Then answer the questions that follow.

The Pine Barrens Tree Frog

1   New Jersey is packed full of people. In fact, it is the most densely populated state in the country. It may seem strange, then, that New Jersey is also home to the largest wilderness area between Boston and Washington, D.C. The Pinelands in southern New Jersey is a large pine forest that includes areas of **bogs**, cedar **swamps**, and winding rivers. Rare plants and animals inhabit the area. One rare species that calls New Jersey home is the tiny, colorful Pine Barrens tree frog.

Appearance

2   This glossy, emerald green frog is just a little over an inch and a half long. The sides and belly are lavender, and a thin white line separates the green and lavender sections. The undersides of its hind legs are bright orange with yellow spots.

Habitat

3   The Pine Barrens tree frog lives in acidic bogs, swamps, and other **wetlands**. It eats small insects and other **invertebrates**. During the early spring breeding season it lays eggs, then attaches them to the bottoms of plants. It only takes three days for dark green tadpoles to hatch from the eggs. The tadpoles grow until they have reached about an inch and a half in length. This usually takes until July or August. Then they **metamorphose** into adult frogs.

4   You might think it would be easy to spot these bright and colorful frogs while visiting the Pinelands. You'd be wrong! For one thing, they're <u>nocturnal</u>. They also spend most of their time under cover. Scientists try to locate them by searching for suitable **habitat** during breeding season. Then they listen for the nasal honking sound of males calling mates on warm, rainy nights. Sometimes the "chorus" of many frogs calling at once can be deafening. Recordings of these frog calls help scientists learn more about their role in the Pinelands **ecosystem**.

The Pine Barrens tree frog also makes its home in other coastal pineland areas. Its usual habitat extends from southern New Jersey to South Carolina, but this tree frog has also been spotted in Alabama and northern Florida.

GO ON

Saving the Tree Frog

5   Even though the Pine Barrens tree frog is relatively common in this special wilderness area, its survival as a species is threatened. This is mainly due to a loss of habitat over the years. Ever since Europeans first settled New Jersey, people have been developing the Pinelands area. They've farmed, cut trees, mined iron, and built structures on it. Development of this kind benefits people but also destroys the natural habitat and breeding grounds of many plants and animals.

6   In the 1970s, the <u>state</u> decided to preserve more than one million acres of the Pinelands as a wilderness area.

This helped stop further loss of animal and plant habitat. People still debate, however, whether the state should prevent or allow development in the Pine Barrens. Some people believe New Jersey citizens should be able to do what they want on the land. Others think the Pinelands and its unique plant and animal life deserve even more protection.

7   The outcome of this debate affects the future of the Pine Barrens tree frog. Allowing people to build houses, roads, mines, and farms on the land would damage the fragile habitat of these animals. Even a slight change in the wetlands water can threaten their survival.

Glossary

bog	a soft, spongy piece of ground that consists mainly of decaying moss and plant material
ecosystem	group of living creatures that interact with one another and their surroundings
habitat	place where a plant or animal naturally lives and grows
invertebrate	without a backbone
metamorphose	to change in form or structure
swamp	a low area of land that is saturated with water
wetland	a swamp, marsh, or bog

15 Knowing that the Latin root *noc* means "night" helps you understand that a nocturnal animal is—

  A active at night.

  B active during the day.

  C as black as night.

  D born during the night.

16 Reread the following sentence from the passage.

In the 1970s, the <u>state</u> decided to preserve more than one million acres of the Pinelands as a wilderness area.

As used in the sentence, *state* means—

A condition.

B political division of a country.

C declare.

D form.

17 Reread the following sentence from the passage.

During the early spring <u>breeding</u> season it lays eggs, then attaches them to the bottoms of plants.

Based on the context of the sentence, the word *breeding* means—

A having to do with green plants.

B having to do with time.

C having to do with reproduction.

D having to do with the seasons.

18 What is MOST likely the purpose for writing this passage?

A to persuade readers to set aside land as wilderness areas

B to inform readers about the Pine Barrens tree frog

C to explain why the tree frog should be saved

D to entertain readers with a story about a tree frog

19 Based upon paragraph 4, we can infer that—

A one of the best ways to find the Pine Barrens tree frog is by listening for their mating call.

B scientists can't record the mating call of the frogs.

C Pine Barrens tree frogs never come out during the day.

D only scientists can find Pine Barrens tree frogs.

20 Where can you find information on the habitat of the Pine Barrens tree frog?

A in the introductory paragraph of the passage

B in the passage, under the heading "Habitat"

C in the diagram

D in the caption that accompanies the diagram

21 The section **Saving the Tree Frog** is developed by—

    A explaining the causes and effects of the loss of the tree frog's habitat.

    B giving reasons why we should save the tree frog.

    C describing the appearance of the tree frog.

    D describing the habitat of the tree frog.

22 A central idea of this passage is that—

    A citizens should be able to do what they want on their land.

    B wetland areas are not good for much except scientific study.

    C the future of the tree frog depends on what happens to its habitat.

    D no more land should be developed in New Jersey.

23 Write a summary of this passage. Be sure to include the main idea and important supporting details from each of the sections. (3 points)

_____

_____

_____

_____

_____

Directions: Read the passages. Then answer the questions that follow.

Dear Parents of Lincoln Middle School Students,

1   The Lincoln Drama Department is currently performing the play *Young Will Shakespeare*. Enclosed is a copy of the review I wrote for our school paper. If you attend one of the upcoming performances, I know you will discover for yourself that this play is a comic masterpiece.

2   Besides being great entertainment, this production is the drama department's only fundraiser this year. That's right, their only request this year is that you purchase tickets and attend this fabulous play! Proceeds from ticket sales will help buy stage equipment and costumes for next year's production.

3   Please join all the Lincoln parents who have already supported our school's drama department. Call the school office to reserve your tickets today!

Sincerely,
Molly Pierce

A Comic Masterpiece

by Molly Pierce

1   When you sit down to watch a play titled *Young Will Shakespeare,* you might expect to see a dramatized version of a dull history book. You'd be mistaken! This performance, directed by Mr. Marshall, is a comic masterpiece that should not be missed.

2   The five-act play is set in Shakespeare's hometown of Stratford-upon-Avon and covers the year of Shakespeare's life just before he headed to London to join a theater company. While some of the details of the play are based on fact, most of the characters are based on characters in Shakespeare's own plays. For example, young Shakespeare's neighbors all resemble characters from his plays *Henry VIII, Romeo and Juliet, and Hamlet.* All these characters and more show up as local figures such as the town butcher, two lovelorn teenagers, and an indecisive mayor.

3   All of the actors are superb in bringing the play to life. Kazuo Kano gives a strong performance as young Will Shakespeare. Marisa Lobel and Ben Jackson are very believable as his parents. The supporting <u>cast</u> members and walk-ons all add great interest to the play. They also keep the pace of the play moving forward.

4   There can be no doubt, however, that the star of the show is assistant director Ray Gonzalez, who bravely tackles the dual roles of Anne Hathaway and Roman (boyfriend of Julia). Casting Ray in the role of a woman was a brilliant decision. In Shakespeare's time, women weren't allowed to act onstage. All of the women's roles were played by boys or young men. Ray's portrayal of Anne Hathaway adds both realism and humor to the play. When I saw the play, the entire audience howled with laughter when Ray fluttered his eyelashes and tried to walk gracefully in a full skirt.

5   Perhaps the greatest moment of all, however, is Ray's scene with Julia, played by Eva Liu. When Ray recites a love poem to her—or should I say squawks a love poem—he reveals his comic genius. The cracking of his voice as he quotes flowery words of love is just perfect. Again, he blends humor with realism. It is no secret that Romeo and Juliet were in their early teens when they fell in love and met their tragic end. The fact that Ray's voice cracks is realistic as well as hysterically funny.

6   *Young Will Shakespeare* seamlessly blends truth and fiction and <u>keeps the audience in stitches</u> as well! This is truly an extraordinary effort by our talented Lincoln students.

24 What information do you learn by reading the letter that you don't find in "A Comic Masterpiece"?

   A The play is directed by Mr. Marshall.

   B The play is a comedy.

   C The main character of the play is William Shakespeare.

   D The play is a fundraiser for the school drama department.

25 Molly Pierce might not be an impartial judge of the play because—

   A she is in the play.

   B she writes for the school paper.

   C she is William Shakespeare's ancestor.

   D she is the daughter of the director.

26 HUMOROUS : FUNNY :: realistic :

   A fictional

   B fantasy

   C drama

   D lifelike

27 Which dictionary definition fits with the meaning of the word *cast* in the following sentence?

The supporting <u>cast</u> members and walk-ons all add great interest to the play.

   A the act of throwing a fishing line

   B the set of actors in a dramatic production

   C something formed by casting in a mold or form

   D the shape or appearance of something

28 The main reason the author wrote the letter is to—

   A entertain readers with a story about Shakespeare.

   B persuade readers to buy tickets for a play.

   C inform readers about Shakespeare's early life.

   D give instructions for producing a school play.

29 The phrase *keeps the audience in stitches* means that the play—

   A hurt the audience.

   B healed the audience.

   C kept the audience laughing.

   D kept the audience quiet.

30 Which statement from the passage is a **fact**?

   A *All of the actors are superb in bringing the play to life.*

   B *Marisa Lobel and Ben Jackson are very believable as his parents.*

   C *Casting Ray in the role of a woman was a brilliant decision.*

   D *In Shakespeare's time, women weren't allowed to act onstage.*

31 Which detail BEST supports Molly Pierce's argument that the play is realistic?

   A Ray Gonzalez's voice cracks when he plays a teen.

   B The role of Julia is played by Eva Liu.

   C The supporting cast keeps the pace moving.

   D Ray Gonzalez is the star of the show.

32 Which detail BEST supports Molly Pierce's argument that the play is humorous?

   A The audience laughed when Ray tried to act like a girl.

   B Kazuo Kano gives a strong performance as young Will Shakespeare.

   C *Young Will Shakespeare* seamlessly blends truth and fiction.

   D Most of the characters are like characters in Shakespeare's own plays.

33 What reasons and evidence does Molly give to support her claim in paragraph 1 of "A Comic Masterpiece" that the play is a comic masterpiece. Evaluate her claims by explaining which reasons are the most convincing to you. (5 points)

_____

_____

_____

_____

_____

> **Take a break. Then go on to Part 3.**

34   The following paragraph contains four pronoun errors. Underline the errors and write the correct pronoun above them. (4 points)

When the football field was damaged by high winds last summer, they decided to have a

clean up day. The football players theirselves picked up the branches on the field. The girls'

track team also got involved. Them picked up the trash on the track. Each girl brought his

own trash bags to save money. By the end of the day, the field and track looked great.

Directions: Read each question and choose the best answer.

---

35   Choose the sentence with the correct capitalization.

_____ is my favorite holiday.

A The Fourth of July
B the Fourth of July
C the fourth of july
D the Fourth of july

36   Choose the sentence with the correct punctuation.

A The supplies needed for art class include the following: watercolors, brushes, charcoal pencils, a drawing pad, and a small canvas.
B The supplies needed for art class include the following; watercolors, brushes, charcoal pencils, a drawing pad, and a small canvas.
C The supplies needed for art class include: the following watercolors, brushes, charcoal pencils, a drawing pad, and a small canvas.
D The supplies needed for art class include the following, watercolors, brushes, charcoal pencils, a drawing pad, and a small canvas.

37   Choose the word that is spelled correctly.

The package _____ eight pounds.

A wade
B wieghed
C weighed
D weide

---

38 Choose the word that is spelled correctly.

A main _____ in his life is to help others.

A principal

B princepal

C principle

D principel

39 Which of the following sentences is an example of standard English grammar?

A I ain't going to walk my dog in the rain.

B Y'all better come to my birthday party.

C He taught hisself to drive the car last summer.

D We aren't going to go on vacation this year.

40 Which sentence is NOT punctuated correctly?

A I never—well, almost never—get up early during summer vacation.

B I have been reading the Hunger Games trilogy (*The Hunger Games, Catching Fire, Mockingjay*).

C The weather, which has been cold and rainy, has not been good for swimming.

D The family—who lives across the street—just put in a swimming pool.

41 Rewrite the following paragraph by combining sentences. Vary sentence patterns for interest. (3 points)

I wanted to get to school early. The bus was late. I stood in the rain and waited. I waited for twenty minutes. The bus came. The bus pulled up to my stop. The bus splashed water all over me. I arrived at school. I was soaking wet. I was late.

_____

_____

_____

_____

_____

_____

STOP

Points Earned / Total = _____ / 60

Keeping Score

	Points Earned / Total Points	Percent Score
Tryout Test	/60	%
Unit One Literature: Key Ideas and Details	/8	%
Unit Two Literature: Craft and Structure	/12	%
Unit Three Literature: Integration of Knowledge and Ideas	/8	%
Unit Four Informational Text: Key Ideas and Details	/8	%
Unit Five Informational Text: Craft and Structure	/12	%
Unit Six Informational Text: Integration of Knowledge and Ideas	/12	%
Unit Seven Language: Pronoun Usage	/8	%
Unit Eight Language: Conventions of Standard English	/8	%
Unit Nine Language: Vocabulary	/8	%
Mastery Test	/60	%

1. Fill in the number of points you earned in the Points Earned box.

2. Use the Finding Percent chart on page 131 to figure out your Percent Score. Then fill in the % box.

3. Compare your Percent Scores for the Tryout Test and the Mastery Test. See how much you've learned!

Common Core Grade 6

Finding Percent

Many tests give your score in both number of points earned and in percentages. This handy chart will tell you your percent score.

1. Find the band with the same number of points that are on your test.
2. Follow along the top row of the band to the number of points you earned. Your percent score is right below it.

Number of Points on Test

8

1	2	3	4	5	6	7	8
13%	25%	38%	50%	63%	75%	88%	100%

12

1	2	3	4	5	6	7	8	9	10	11	12
8%	17%	25%	33%	42%	50%	58%	67%	75%	83%	92%	100%

60

1	2	3	4	5	6	7	8	9	10	11	12	13	14	15	16	17
2%	3%	5%	7%	8%	10%	12%	13%	15%	17%	18%	20%	22%	23%	25%	27%	28%

18	19	20	21	22	23	24	25	26	27	28	29	30	31	32	33	34
30%	32%	33%	35%	37%	38%	40%	42%	43%	45%	47%	48%	50%	52%	53%	55%	57%

35	36	37	38	39	40	41	42	43	44	45	46	47	48	49	50	51
58%	60%	62%	63%	65%	67%	68%	70%	72%	73%	75%	77%	78%	80%	82%	83%	85%

52	53	54	55	56	57	58	59	60
87%	88%	90%	93%	94%	95%	97%	99%	100%

WRITING TEST WORKSHOPS

Writing Test Workshops

To the Student

Why Do I Need This Book?

This book will help you practice taking writing tests. You will learn how to—

- read a writing prompt
- get your ideas down on paper
- write a narrative
- write to explain
- write about an opinion

How Will My Writing Be Scored?

Your writing test will be scored by test readers who use rubrics, or scoring guides. The rubric below lists six qualities of good writing. Read through each characteristic so you know how your writing will be graded.

Rubric Score: *1* is the lowest; *5* is the highest					
Ideas/Content—focuses on one main idea; the details add to the main idea	①	②	③	④	⑤
Organization—has a clear beginning, middle, and end; the order is easy to follow	①	②	③	④	⑤
Voice—communicates feelings and personality; the writing is unique	①	②	③	④	⑤
Word Choice—uses colorful, fresh words in the right places	①	②	③	④	⑤
Sentence Fluency—uses both long and short sentences that flow smoothly	①	②	③	④	⑤
Conventions—few or no spelling, capitalization, and punctuation errors	①	②	③	④	⑤

How to Manage Your Time During an Essay Test

You may have only 20 to 45 minutes to complete a writing test so it's important to have a plan.

If you have 20 minutes,

◎ read the prompt, circle key ideas, brainstorm, and organize ideas (5 minutes)

◎ write the essay (10 minutes)

◎ edit and proofread (5 minutes)

How to Read a Writing Prompt

A *prompt* is the assignment for a writing test. The prompt gives you directions. It also tells you what to write about.

> ◎ **Step 1**
>
> Read through the entire prompt. Decide what the topic is.
>
> ◎ **Step 2**
>
> Read through the prompt a second time, underlining key words (*explain, compare, tell*) that will help you focus your writing.
>
> ◎ **Step 3**
>
> Look for key words or phrases you might use in your main idea statement.

Emilio's Prompt

Here is a prompt for Emilio's test. Look at the key words he underlined. They helped Emilio understand exactly what he was supposed to do.

Sample Prompt

Your school board <u>is considering having schools go to a four-day week.</u> A four-day school week would require that <u>75 minutes be added to the end of the day.</u> Before the school board makes a decision, it would like to hear from the public. <u>Write a letter expressing your opinion, supported with convincing reasons.</u>

The prompt tells Emilio that he must write a persuasive letter. His main idea will be his opinion on a four-day school week and will most likely include words such as *should* or *should not*. Finally, he will need to include reasons to support his opinion.

Try It On Your Own

Read the prompt below. Underline any key words and phrases that might be helpful to you as a writer.

Prompt

A leading doctor claims that to do their best in school, students under 16 should get 11 hours of sleep at night. Based on her advice, your parents are considering making your bedtime 8:00. You disagree. Write a letter to your parents that explains your position.

Argumentative Writing Tests

Argumentative Writing

Review the Standards (W.6.1.a–e, W.6.4, W.6.5)

- Write **arguments** to support **claims** with clear **reasons** and relevant **evidence**
- Produce clear and coherent writing appropriate to task, purpose, and audience
- Develop and strengthen writing by planning, revising, editing, and rewriting

Argumentative writing is focused on developing an **argument** to convince your reader that your opinion is right. You make a **claim**, and then you use **reasons** and **evidence** to support your claim.

Introduction

- state your main idea (claim) in one sentence

Cutting the sixth-grade drama program would hurt the quality of education for students at our school.

Body

- develop your argument with clear reasons and relevant evidence

Reason: Participating in school plays gives students confidence to speak in front of people.

Evidence: Many jobs require people to speak in front of both small and large groups of people.

Good reasons are—

- based on logic
- supported with evidence such as facts, quotations from experts, and examples

Emotional appeals—

- use emotion to motivate the reader
- are not as persuasive as logical reasons
- should be used sparingly
- are most effective in the introduction and conclusion

Conclusion

- restate the main idea
- review reasons
- end with a strong thought

In conclusion, I believe that any cuts to our drama program would hurt the students at our school.

Alex's Prompt

Below is a prompt that Alex was given on a writing test. Notice the key words Alex underlined in the prompt.

Prompt

Your school district is considering requiring all fifth- and sixth-grade students to take band. Instruments would be rented at a reasonable fee for those who did not want to purchase them. What is your opinion of such a requirement? Write an argument stating your viewpoint and supporting it with convincing reasons.

First, Alex decided whether he was for or against all students having to take band in fifth and sixth grades. Then he organized his ideas about the issue. Look at the organizer Alex created. Notice that he placed a star next to the most important ideas.

Issue: Whether fifth- and sixth-grade students should be required to take band

Main Idea/Claim: Requiring all fifth- and sixth-grade students to take band would be difficult for both the families and schools.

Reasons/Evidence

Students get enough music in music class.

Some students may already be taking instrumental lessons.

★ Some families may not be able to afford to rent an instrument./Instruments can cost thousands of dollars.

Band concerts could interfere with other activities.

★ Some students have no interest in music. Only one-fourth of sixth-graders currently take band.

★ Extra band teachers would have to be hired.

Words you might find in a prompt that requires you to write persuasively

agree, disagree
argue, argument
convince
opinion

oppose
position
should
should not

stand
support

Alex's Writing

Requirements! Requirements! Requirements! Students get more requirements thrown at them every year. They're so busy doing the required things that they don't have time to choose what they want to do. Requiring all fifth and sixth grade students to take band would be difficult for both families and schools.

One reason these students should not have to take band is that some kids just don't have an interest in music. Music is not for everybody. I have a lot of friends who don't even like going to music class. They would really hate being forced to take band! Some students are more into sports or dance or scouting. Making these students take band would be a waste of time because they wouldn't like it.

Another reason is that some parents might not be able to afford the instrument rental. Some families don't make much moola. They don't have a lot to spend on things like musical instruments. They have enough to do to pay their bills. I have a friend in sixth grade who has a brother in fifth grade. Their parents would have to pay two rentals. How fair would that be?

My final reason is because the district would have to hire at least one more band teacher. Their are three fifth and four sixth grades at our school. That's almost 200 students. Ain't no way Ms. Jenkins could handle that many kids in one day! That means one or two teachers would have to be hired. Everyone's always talking about how the school doesn't have any money. Then how could it afford to hire more teachers?

Fifth and sixth grade students should not be required to take band. Period.

Looking at Alex's Writing

- Does Alex's introduction grab your attention? Why or why not?

- Circle Alex's main idea. Is his claim clearly stated?

- Underline the reasons Alex has included that support his main idea. Now look back at his organizer. Are these his strongest reasons?

- Put a check mark next to places where you think Alex uses an inappropriate style to express his ideas.

- Mark and correct any problems in mechanics (spelling, capitalization, punctuation, and grammar).

- Underline Alex's concluding statement. Could it be improved?

Try It On Your Own

Directions: Now it's your turn to write an argument. Follow the steps in order. If your teacher gives you a time limit, make a plan by filling in the amount of minutes you have to complete each step.

Step 1—Read the prompt and underline any key words. (_____ minutes)
Step 2—Brainstorm for ideas on a separate piece of paper. (_____ minutes)
Step 3—Fill in the graphic organizer to help you organize your paper. (_____ minutes)

Time Allowed

_____ minutes

Prompt

A litter problem has developed at your school. Students are throwing trash on the ground and leaving empty cans and bottles outside on benches. Your principal has asked students to pick up after themselves, but the litter problem continues. The principal has reacted by canceling all after-school activities until the problem is taken care of and stays taken care of for two weeks. What is your position on this issue? Write an argument that includes a claim. Support your claim with good reasons and evidence.

Issue: _____
Main Idea/Claim: _____
Reasons/Evidence

GO ON →

Step 4—Using the organizer as a guide, write your essay on a separate piece of paper. Be sure to include an introduction and conclusion. (_____ minutes)

Step 5—Go back and proofread your paper for mistakes in capitalization, punctuation, and grammar. (_____ minutes)

Step 6—Now evaluate your own writing (or ask a friend to evaluate your paper).

How Did You Do?

Directions: Complete the following tasks. Then fill in the rubric below.

1. **Ideas/Content** Underline your main idea/claim.
   - Number the reasons that support your position statement. (1, 2, 3, etc.)
   - Put a check mark by your strongest reason.
   - Put an E by evidence used to support your reasons.

2. **Organization** Can you identify the introduction and conclusion? Write **I** and **C** next to them.
   - Put a box around linking words such as *first*, *next*, *second*, *finally*, and *also*.

3. **Voice** Does the writing communicate a positive, confident attitude, or does the writer seem angry or sound like a know-it-all?

4. **Word Choice** Circle any words that seem especially fresh or vivid.
   - Cross out any words that are not exciting or precise. Also cross out any slang or language that is too informal.

5. **Sentence Fluency** Put a check next to any sentences that seem too choppy or too long.
   - Try combining sentences that are too short or creating two sentences from an overly long one.

6. **Conventions** Check for any errors in spelling, capitalization, and punctuation.

Rubric
Score: *1* is the lowest; *5* is the highest

Ideas/Content—focuses on one main idea; the details add to the main idea	①	②	③	④	⑤
Organization—has a clear beginning, middle, and end; the order is easy to follow	①	②	③	④	⑤
Voice—communicates feelings and personality; the writing is unique	①	②	③	④	⑤
Word Choice—uses colorful, fresh words in the right places	①	②	③	④	⑤
Sentence Fluency—uses both long and short sentences that flow smoothly	①	②	③	④	⑤
Conventions—few or no spelling, capitalization, and punctuation errors	①	②	③	④	⑤

One way I can improve my writing is by _____

_____

Informative Writing Tests

Informative Writing

Review the Standards (W.6.2.a–f, W.6.4, W.6.5)
- Write **informative**/explanatory texts with an **introduction** and **conclusion**
- Develop the topic with facts and **details**
- Use appropriate **transitions** and precise language
- Use a formal style

When you write a paper about an insect you studied in science class or a group of people you studied in social studies, you are writing to inform or explain. You are also writing to inform when you tell how to swing a bat or start a rock collection. This type of writing is also called *expository writing*.

A piece of informative writing normally has three parts: an introduction, a body, and a conclusion.

Introduction
- grabs the reader's attention
- states the main idea

Whack! Alex Rodriguez hits another home run—and so effortlessly! But Rodriguez wasn't born with that graceful swing. It came from years and years of hard practice. Swinging a bat looks easy, but to do it right takes skill.

> **"Hook" your reader by—**
> - *giving a surprising fact*
> - *telling them a story*
> - *asking a question*

Body
- contains **details** that support your main idea
- is organized in a logical order
- uses good **transition** words (*first, next, after, finally*)

First, you must have the right stance. Your feet should be parallel to the plate. More weight should be on your back foot than on your front foot.

Conclusion
- summarizes the main idea and supporting points

Keep in mind that, in order to be a good batter, you have to stand correctly, hold the bat right, and concentrate.

- ends with a strong thought

With a few years of hard practice, you could be the next Alex Rodriguez!

Ellery's Prompt

Below is the writing prompt Ellery was given on a test.

Prompt

Everyone has an idea of what he or she would like to do when they grow up. What career are you considering? Write a paper <u>explaining the career you would like to have someday</u>. Provide <u>at least three reasons why</u> you are considering this career. <u>Include specific details to explain your reasons.</u>

Ellery created the following web to help organize her ideas before she started to write. Notice that she placed the subject—zoo veterinarian—in the top circle. She listed reasons for wanting to be a zoo veterinarian in the next three circles. Finally, she jotted down a few details to explain each of her reasons.

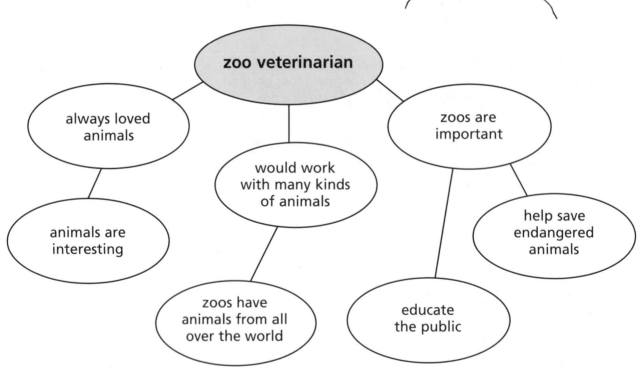

As you read Ellery's writing, look for proof of the planning she did.

Ellery's Writing

Slowly the stalker approachs the rhinoceros. she raises her gun and fires. Pffft! A few seconds later the big beast drops with a thud! Dead? No, sleeping. The "stalker" is a zoo veterinarian, and her gun is a dart gun used to put animals to sleep for medical treetment. Someday I'm going to be that zoo veterinarian!

One reason I want to be a zoo vet is because I love animals. When I was really lettle, I used to drag home every stray dog and cat—and some that weren't strays. There was only one dog I didn't like. Our neighbor's German shepherd. He was mean.

I also want to be a zoo veterinarian is because I would get to work with different animals. from all over the world. Sometimes a zoo in the United States will trade animals with a zoo from another country. This is so they can each learn about animals from other countries. And zoos don't just have mammals. They also have birds insects fish reptiles and amphibians. I hope someday to work with them all—except the insects. I don't think zoo vets do a lot with insects, which is good because I can't stand those huge cockroaches they have at zoos now! Yuck!

Finally, I've liked to be a veterinarian at a zoo because I think zoos are important. Zoos help educate the public about wildlife. They teach people about endangered animals too, and they help save them. Endangered animals are raised at zoos, and then released into the wild when there are enough of them. Zoos perform important jobs today.

My goal has always been to be a zoo veterinarian. As long as I don't have to work with those cockroaches, that is!

GO ON

Looking at Ellery's Writing

- Place an *M* by the main idea.
- Place an *S* by each supporting reason.
- Cross out the details that don't support the main idea.
- Circle two transitional words or phrases.
- Add one or two sentences to improve Ellery's conclusion.
- Mark and correct any mistakes in spelling, capitalization, punctuation, and grammar.

Try It On Your Own

Now it's your turn to take a practice writing test. Follow the steps in order. If your teacher gives you a time limit, make a plan by filling in the amount of minutes you have to complete each step.

_____
minutes

Step 1—Read the prompt and underline any key words.
(_____ minutes)

Step 2—Brainstorm for ideas on a separate piece of paper.
(_____ minutes)

Step 3—Fill in the graphic organizer to help you organize your paper.
(_____ minutes)

Prompt

The U.S. Postal Service has honored many individuals by putting their pictures on postage stamps. Whom would you nominate to put on a postage stamp? The person can be someone you know or someone you have heard about. He or she can be living or dead or even a fictional character. Write a paper indicating whom you would choose, and why that person deserves to be put on a postage stamp. Support your ideas with details.

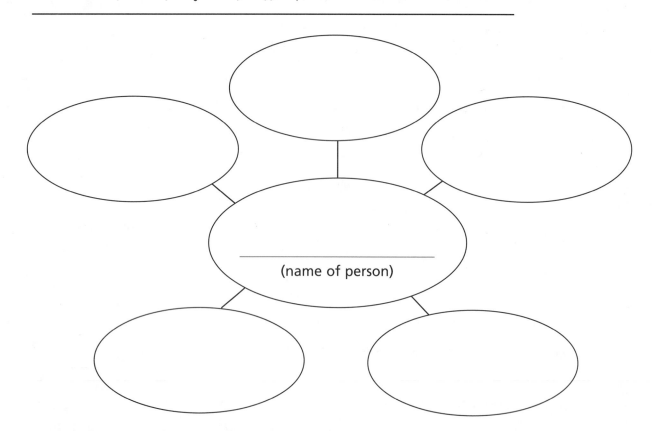

(name of person)

Step 4—Using the organizer as a guide, write your paper on a separate piece of paper. Be sure to include an introduction and conclusion. (_____ minutes)

Step 5—Go back and proofread your paper for mistakes in capitalization, punctuation, and grammar. (_____ minutes)

How Did You Do?

Directions: Complete the following tasks. Then fill in the rubric below.

1. **Ideas/Content** Is your main idea clear? Underline your main idea.
   - Number the details that support your main idea. (1, 2, 3, etc.)
2. **Organization** Can you identify the introduction and conclusion? Write **I** and **C** next to them.
   - Put a box around linking words such as *first*, *next*, *second*, *finally*, and *also*.
3. **Voice** Does the writing communicate a positive, confident tone? Put a **V** next to any sections where the voice doesn't fit with the topic.
4. **Word Choice** Circle any words that seem especially fresh or vivid. Cross out any words that are boring, slang, or informal English.
5. **Sentence Fluency** Put a check mark next to any sentences that seem too choppy or too long.
6. **Conventions** Check for any errors in spelling, capitalization, and punctuation.

Rubric Score: *1* is the lowest; *5* is the highest					
Ideas/Content—focuses on one main idea; the details add to the main idea	①	②	③	④	⑤
Organization—has a clear beginning, middle, and end; the order is easy to follow	①	②	③	④	⑤
Voice—communicates feelings and personality; the writing is unique	①	②	③	④	⑤
Word Choice—uses colorful, fresh words in the right places	①	②	③	④	⑤
Sentence Fluency—uses both long and short sentences that flow smoothly	①	②	③	④	⑤
Conventions—few or no spelling, capitalization, and punctuation errors	①	②	③	④	⑤

One way I can improve my writing is by _____

_____

_____

Narrative Writing

Review the Standards (W.6.3.a–e, W.6.4, W.6.5)

- Write **narratives** about real or imaginary events
- Introduce **characters**
- Use **dialogue**, **pacing**, **description**, and **transitional words**
- Provide a conclusion

When you tell your friend what you did at your cousin's house last summer or when you make up an adventure to tell your little brother or sister at bedtime, you are telling a story, or **narrative**.

A good story needs a beginning, a middle, and an ending.

Beginning

- introduces the **characters**, setting, and a problem or conflict
- may also give a personal evaluation of the real-life events:

The day my best friend moved away was the worst day of my life.

Middle

- develops the plot or the events that happen
- tells events in time order
- includes appropriate **transitional words** and phrases (*next*, *afterward*, *when we said good-bye*)
- includes interesting **dialogue** and **description**
- maintains appropriate **pace** (not too fast or too slow)

Description—precise, lively words:

The sky turned gray as I pedaled my bike down the gravel path.

Ending

- provides the ending for your story
- explains how the experience changed you
- ends with a strong thought that may include what you learned about the experience:

I've had a lot of friends since then, but a friend like Mara comes around only once in a lifetime.

"What's **dialogue**?" Joey asked.

"It's talking between characters," Mia replied.

Joey said with a laugh, "Oh, like what we're doing right now!"

Keio's Prompt

Below is the prompt Keio was given on a writing test. Help her out by underlining the key words for her.

Prompt ——————————————————————

Life has a way of teaching us lessons when we least expect it. Recall an experience you've had that taught you a valuable lesson. Tell the story of that incident.

——————————————————————

Keio began by mapping out her story. Look at the story map she created for the above prompt.

Words you might find in a narrative writing prompt

event	relate
experience	remember
incident	story
narrate	tell
recall	time

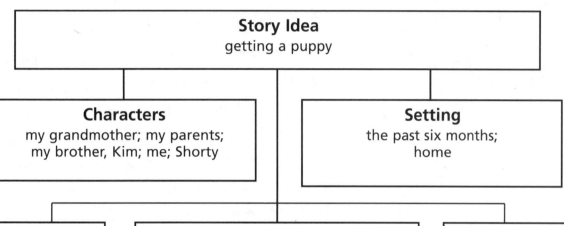

Story Idea
getting a puppy

Characters
my grandmother; my parents; my brother, Kim; me; Shorty

Setting
the past six months; home

Beginning
my grandmother's warning

Middle
my brother and me begging for a puppy; our move to Somerville; getting Shorty; living with Shorty

End
what I learned

Look for proof of the planning Keio did as you read her story.

- Find and underline Keio's main idea statement.

- How well did Keio's hook grab your attention?

- Circle any background information Keio provides for her readers. Do you think that information is necessary to understand the main point of the story?

- Put a star by any details Keio provides about her characters. What additional details might she have provided?

Keio's Story

"Be careful what you wish for," my grandmother always told me. "Because you might just get it and THEN . . ." Grandmother never finished her sentence, and I never really thought much about what she meant. What could be wrong with getting what you wish for? If you wish for something, you must want it. And if you want it, it must be something good, right? Not always. Getting what I wished for last year taught me that my grandmother was right.

My brother, Kim, and I had always wanted a puppy. We begged our parents, but they always told us "no" because we lived in an apartment. But six months ago when we moved to Somerville, we bought a house with a fenced yard. So, of course, Kim and I started begging for a puppy again. At first our parents said no, but after a few weeks, we finally wore them down.

"All right, we'll get a puppy," Dad said. "But I have to warn you. A puppy's a big responsibility. Someone has to feed him and give him water. And he'll need to be taken for walks."

"That's right," Mom agreed. "And puppies make messes. It'll be up to the two of you to clean up after him."

"I will! I will!" I remember yelling gleefully.

"So will I!" Kim said. "Keio and I will do *everything*!"

Little did we know how much we would regret our promises.

The next day we went to the animal shelter and adopted a puppy that was part-beagle and part-dachshund. We named him Shorty because his legs were only about an inch long. Now I think we should have named him Messy.

The first mess Shorty made was in the car on the way home. I guess the car ride didn't agree with him. Everything he'd eaten for breakfast came up on the floor mat. I cheerfully volunteered to clean it up. After all, who could blame him? And it was only one mess. The second mess Shorty made happened in a corner in the living room about five minutes after we got him home. This time it was Kim's turn to clean up. Thank goodness!

If I listed all the messes Shorty has made in the time that we've had him, this would be a novel. Let's just say that he's always into trouble. But worst of all, he's not even close to being housebroken!

Having Shorty has taught me that you really DO have to be careful what you wish for. Just because something seems good at the time doesn't mean that it is good.

Looking at Keio's Story

- Draw a box around any transitional words or phrases Keio uses.

- Is Keio's story a manageable size? Yes _____ No _____

- Label the beginning, middle, and ending of Keio's story (B, M, and E). Are the events provided in the correct time order?

GO ON

Try It On Your Own

Directions: It's your turn to write a story. Read the prompt below. Then underline the key words and phrases.

Step 1—Read the prompt and underline any key words. (_____ minutes)

Prompt

Everyone has good days that he or she remembers. Think of one of the best days you've ever had. Tell the story of that day. Provide details that will help readers understand the good things that happened to you that day.

Step 2—Brainstorm for ideas on a separate piece of paper. (_____ minutes)

Step 3—Fill in the graphic organizer to help you organize your paper. (_____ minutes)

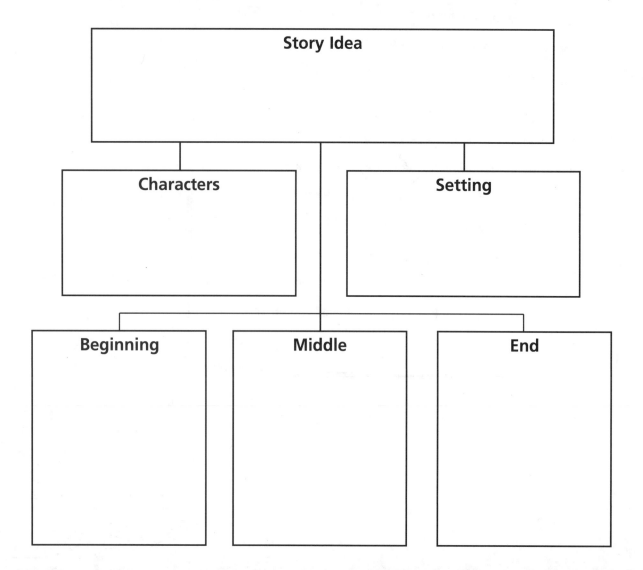

Step 4—Using the organizer as a guide, write your story on a separate piece of paper. (_____ minutes)

Step 5—Go back and proofread your paper for mistakes in capitalization, punctuation, and grammar. (_____ minutes)

Step 6—Now evaluate your own writing (or ask a friend to evaluate your story).

How Did You Do?

Directions: Complete the following tasks. Then fill in the rubric below.

1. **Ideas/Content** Underline the sentence that contains the main problem or conflict in the story. Put a check by any events that stray away from the main problem. Put a smiley face next to good description or dialogue.

2. **Organization** Identify the beginning, middle, and ending of the story by writing **B**, **M**, and **E** next to where you find them in the story. Put a box around linking words such as *later, next, then*, and *after*.

3. **Voice** Put a **V** next to any part of the story where the writer's personality shines through the writing.

4. **Word Choice** Circle any words that seem especially fresh or vivid. Cross out any words that are boring or not precise.

5. **Sentence Fluency** Put a wavy line under any sentences that seem too choppy or too long.

6. **Conventions** Check for any errors in spelling, capitalization, and punctuation.

Rubric Score: *1* lowest; *5* is the highest					
Ideas/Content—focuses on one main idea; the details add to the main idea	①	②	③	④	⑤
Organization—has a clear beginning, middle, and end; the order is easy to follow	①	②	③	④	⑤
Voice—communicates feelings and personality; the writing is unique	①	②	③	④	⑤
Word Choice—uses colorful, fresh words in the right places	①	②	③	④	⑤
Sentence Fluency—uses both long and short sentences that flow smoothly	①	②	③	④	⑤
Conventions—few or no spelling, capitalization, and punctuation errors	①	②	③	④	⑤

One way I can improve my writing is by _____

_____

_____

Research Writing Tests

Research Reports

Review the Standards (W.6.4, W.6.5, W.6.7, W.6.8)

- Conduct short research projects
- Draw evidence from literary or informational texts to support research

Sometimes a writing test or performance task will require you to conduct research and then write a research report. These types of testing events may take place over several days. You will be given time to go to the media center or computer lab.

A research report is organized much like an informational or argumentative essay.

Introduction
- gets the reader's attention
- contains the main idea

Body
- gives details that support the main idea
- contains good transitional words and phrases

Conclusion
- restates the main idea
- summarizes supporting details
- ends with a strong thought

Allie's Prompt

Below is a prompt that Allie was given as a writing task. Notice the key words she underlined.

Prompt

Your school is considering putting up a wind turbine next to the athletic fields to help supply the school with electricity. Conduct research on wind power and then write an essay explaining how a wind turbine works and the benefits of using wind power. Be sure to include three sources in your final paper. At least one source should be from a book or a periodical, such as a newspaper or magazine.

www.photos.com

Allie turned the underlined ideas from the prompt into questions to guide her research. Then she organized her notes according to the questions, being sure to keep careful track of the sources she used.

How does a wind turbine work?	What are the benefits to our school having a wind turbine?
The wind turns the propeller-like blades around a rotor. As the rotor moves, it turns the drive shaft, which runs an electric generator. —"Wind Power." www.energysavers.gov	Wind power doesn't pollute. Wind power contributes to a better environment by producing clean power, a stronger economy by creating wind power-related employment, and greater energy security by providing a domestic source of energy. —"Wind Power." www.energysavers.gov/your_home
The generator sends the power to a sub-station. —"Alternative Energy." www.energyrefuge.com	A school in Spirit Lake, IA has their own wind farm. Two wind turbines tower over the playground. They are expected to provide about $140,000 in annual energy savings in 2011. —Kessler, Barbara. "Growing New Energy: How Iowa Raced Ahead in Wind Power." www.greenrightnow.com 10 September 2010
The tower is hollow and made of steel. The blades are made of fiberglass and polyester. Many wind turbines are between 200 to 300 feet tall. —"Wind Power." www.alliantenergykids.com	Tippecanoe Valley School Corp. is building a 321-foot-high PowerWind turbine, on school property. A wind turbine with behind-the-meter technology will provide about 70 percent of all electrical power used on the campus. The school received a grant from the federal government to finance the project. The students at the school will learn about wind power and energy as part of their curriculum. —Slone, David. "Valley Breaks Ground on Wind Turbine." www.timesuniononline.com, 6 June 2011
Blades are around 160 feet long. —"Wind Turbines." www.hybridynepower.com	
With behind-the-meter technology, a school can capture all of the electricity generated by its wind turbines and store it for the school to use as needed. Often this technology uses solar power as well. —"Wind Turbine Quick Facts." www.midamericanenergy.com	"Through the Wind for Schools project, funded by the Department of Energy, our school received a grant from the Department of Energy, Wind, and Water program's Wind Powering America initiative. Students at our school will have access to the data generated by the wind turbine. This project will benefit our school both financially and educationally." —Interview with Principal Maria Garza

Evaluating Sources

Use the following questions to evaluate a source.

Who is the authority? Make sure the author and the Web site are from reliable, credible sources. Are the writers experts on the subject? Watch for .gov or .edu at the end of the address. These indicate that the source is from a government agency or educational body.

Who's behind it? Is the source from a business or group that has a reason for promoting some information and withholding other facts?

When was it written? A pamphlet may be from your state government, but if it was published in 1990, the information is out-of-date.

Next, Allie used the following graphic organizer to organize her report. Notice how she used the prompt to write her main idea statement.

Main Idea: Building a wind turbine would benefit our school and our planet.

Detail: How wind power works

Facts/Evidence: What turbines look like
- over 200 feet tall; blades 200 to 300 feet
- tower is made of steel
- blades made of fiberglass and polyester

Detail: How energy is produced

Facts/Evidence:
- Wind powers the blades, running an electric generator
- Generator sends power to a grid where it is stored for use by the school
- Could also use solar power to increase efficiency

Detail: Benefits

Facts/Evidence:
- Clean power; doesn't pollute, unlike oil or coal
- Financial savings to school
- Tippecanoe Valley School
- Educational benefits
- Interview with principal Maria Garza

www.photos.com

Allie's Report

Two of the biggest problems in America today is a lack of money for education and our dependence upon energy forms that hurt the environment. Our school is considering a way to help with both of these problems. They are considering installing a wind turbine around the school's athletic fields. Building a wind turbine would benefit our school and our planet.

You've probably seen huge wind turbines as you've driven across the country. More and more wind farms are cropping up across America. The steel tower is often over 200 feet tall. The fiberglass and polyester blades can be another 200 feet long. That's really tall ("Wind Power")!

As wind turns the blades of the windmill, the center, or rotor, moves, turning a drive shaft. The drive shaft runs an electric generator that makes the electricity. This electricity can then be sent to a sub-station where anyone can use it or it can be stored for use by our school. Some schools use a combination of solar power and wind power ("Wind Turbines").

Our school would benefit in many ways from wind energy. First, it would help the planet. Because the wind is a clean energy source. Burning coal or oil for electricity pollutes the air.

There would also be a financial savings to the school. Tippecanoe Valley School in Warsaw, Indiana, is building a 321-foot-high turbine on their property. Wind power is expected to generate about 70 percent of the electricity the school needs (Slone). This is a huge saving to the school. Spirit Lake schools in Iowa expect to save $140,000 on energy costs due

Looking at Allie's Report

- Underline Allie's main idea statement.
- Does Allie's order make sense?
  Yes _____ No _____
- Circle any transitional words and phrases.
- Does she give credit to the sources she used?
  Yes _____ No _____
- Do her sources seem reliable and credible?
  Yes _____ No _____

GO ON

to their two wind turbines (Kessler).

Our school would benefit from wind power educationally. Science classes could study the wind turbines and learn how they produce energy. This would be a great way to learn about green energy. Our administrator Maria Garza said, "This project will benefit our school both financially and educationally."

There are many benefits to our school having a wind turbine. Grants are available from the government to help with the cost. Now is a great time to save the planet and save our school some money. I think it would be really cool thing for our school to do.

Looking at Allie's Report

- Does she meet the requirement of using at least three sources with one source from a book or periodical?

  Yes _____ No _____

- Cross out any slang or informal language.

- Mark and correct any problems in mechanics (spelling, capitalization, punctuation, and grammar).

Try It On Your Own

Step 1—Read the prompt below. Then underline key words and phrases.

Prompt

Your friends are upset because the school has instituted a new policy removing all sugary snacks, desserts, and drinks from lunches and vending machines. Write an essay explaining why too much sugar is not good for kids. Conduct research to use in your paper. Be sure to include information from at least three different sources.

Step 2—Turn the information from the prompt into questions to guide your research. Write your question(s) below.

_____

_____

_____

_____

Step 3—Conduct research to answer the questions. Be sure to use the guidelines given in the prompt. Keep your research organized by including the source information next to your notes.

Step 4—Fill in the graphic organizer with your main idea and supporting details.

Step 5—Using the organizer as a guide, write your report on a separate piece of paper. Be sure to cite your sources when you use them in your paper.

Step 6—Go back and proofread your paper for mistakes in capitalization, punctuation, and grammar.

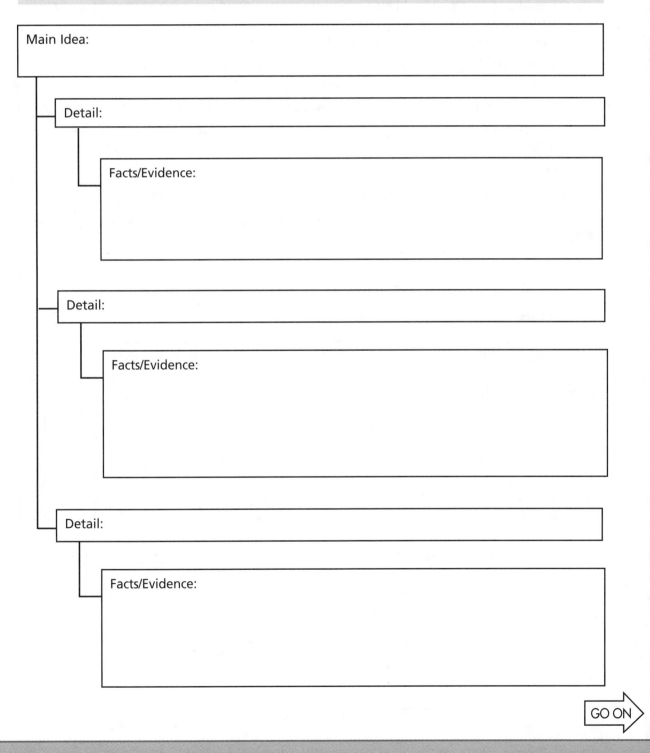

Main Idea:

Detail:

Facts/Evidence:

Detail:

Facts/Evidence:

Detail:

Facts/Evidence:

GO ON

How Did You Do?

Directions: Complete the following tasks. Then fill in the rubric below.

---

1. **Ideas/Content** Underline your main idea.
   - Number the details that support your main idea. (1, 2, 3, etc.)
   - Does the report meet the requirements of the prompt? Yes ____ No ____
   - Does your paper include information from at least three sources? Yes ____ No __
   - Write *citation* next to any passages that are missing a citation.

2. **Organization** Can you identify the introduction and conclusion? Write **I** and **C** next to them.
   - Put a box around transitional words such as *first, next, second, finally,* and *also.*

3. **Voice** Does the writing communicate a confident, formal voice? Yes ____ No ____

4. **Word Choice** Circle any words that seem especially fresh or vivid.
   - Cross out any words that are slang or too informal for a research report.

5. **Sentence Fluency** Put a check next to any sentences that seem too choppy or too long.

6. **Conventions** Are quotation marks used with direct quotations? Yes ____ No ____
   - Check for any errors in spelling, capitalization, and punctuation.

Rubric
Score: *1* lowest; *5* is the highest

Ideas/Content—focuses on one main idea; the details add to the main idea; appropriate sources are used	①	②	③	④	⑤
Organization—has a clear beginning, middle, and end; the order is easy to follow	①	②	③	④	⑤
Voice—communicates feelings and personality; the writing is unique	①	②	③	④	⑤
Word Choice—uses colorful, fresh words in the right places	①	②	③	④	⑤
Sentence Fluency—uses both long and short sentences that flow smoothly	①	②	③	④	⑤
Conventions—few or no spelling, capitalization, and punctuation errors	①	②	③	④	⑤

One way I can improve my writing is by _____

_____

_____